AMERICAN HOUSE STYLES

A CONCISE GUIDE

Also by John Milnes Baker

How to Build a House with an Architect

AMERICAN HOUSE STYLES

A CONCISE GUIDE

JOHN MILNES BAKER, A.I.A.

W. W. NORTON & COMPANY
New York   London

ACKNOWLEDGMENTS

Special thanks to Clarkson N. Potter, Helga Maass Potter, Kate Delano Condax, Susan Elia, and Barclay Morrison. They all know the help they gave me on this book and I am extremely grateful. I also want to thank James L. Mairs and Cecil Lyon of W. W. Norton for their patience, encouragement, and support, and Nancy Palmquist for her care and judgment in editing my manuscript.

My appreciation to Eugene Raskin for sharing his insights and observations on the sociology of architecture. I have never been sure where his views stop and mine begin.

I also want to acknowledge my debt and gratitude to the late Paul Wescott, who introduced the history of architecture to The Hill School in Pottstown, Pennsylvania; his survey course was unique in secondary schools. I have never taken a course anywhere that had a greater influence on my life. He deserves much credit for this book.

Printed in the United States of America
Composition by The Sarabande Press, New York, New York
Book design and illustrations by John Milnes Baker

Library of Congress Cataloging-in-Publication Data

Baker, John Milnes, 1932–
    American house styles : a concise guide / John Milnes Baker.
        p.   cm.
    Includes bibliographical references and index.
    1. Architecture, Domestic—United States—Themes, motives.
    I. Title.
NA7205.B33   1933
728'.37'0973—dc20   92—42937

ISBN: 978-0-393-32325-2

W. W. Norton & Company, Inc.
500 Fifth Avenue, New York, N.Y. 10110
www.wwnorton.com

W. W. Norton & Company Ltd.
Castle House, 75/76 Wells Street, London W1T 3QT

2 3 4 5 6 7 8 9 0

This book is dedicated to my wife, Liddy, for her untiring support and her capacity for insightful comments and cheerful help while still managing her own career and a household that often resembles a bed and breakfast operation.

By and large [Renaissance] architects promoted that unity of creative expression in any given country and period that we call style.

—Hugh Morrison, *Early American Architecture*, 1952

PREFACE

Many books have been written on architectural styles—some dealing specifically with houses. All tend to identify particular styles and invariably show representative examples of actual buildings. The diversity of scale and building types, however, often diverts the focus from the elements of the style to the type of building shown. The salt-box, the Cape Cod, the octagon, the suburban four-square, and the bungalow are often treated as styles when in fact they are really building types. The subject can become very confusing.

Stylistic embellishments of American houses have tended to be superficial veneers that often veiled inventive floor plans and commonsense designs for new American living patterns. The "content," as distinct from the "style," was apt to be more innovative than one might suppose at first glance. This difference between style and content—between the clothes and the person—is obviated by the use of the same basic house plan throughout this guide.

As an architect who specializes in residential design, I can do something that most architectural writers cannot: I can design a simple two-story house with four bedrooms that would meet the needs of a family today, and I can develop this basic plan in almost any number of historical styles. By this technique, the essential characteristics of a given style can be emphasized in each version of the house.

The house plan used throughout this guide is basically a 44-foot by 32-foot rectangle. The ground floor includes a front entrance hall and stairway, a living room, a dining room, and a kitchen with a good-sized family sitting area. There is also a mudroom entry with ample closets, a laundry room, a powder room, and convenient access to the basement level. Four bedrooms are located on the second floor and are arranged for convenience and privacy. The house is about 3,000 square feet and would have a garage connected at the mudroom entrance.

The elements of the style—the massing, scale, proportion, and character derived from the nature of the building materials, details, and spatial flow—will all vary widely in the examples that follow.

Even people interested in houses can rarely identify the style of their own homes with any precision. I hope this book will stimulate an interest in looking at architecture, particularly houses, with a new perspective and will help develop the basis for an informed critical

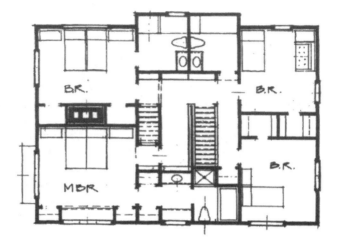

SECOND FLOOR

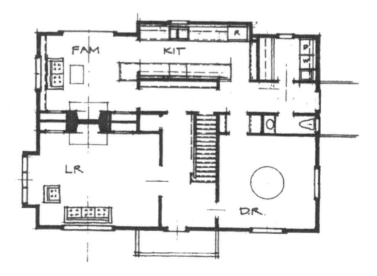

GROUND FLOOR
Scale: $^1/_{16}'' = 1'\text{-}0''$

assessment of our man-made world. "Colonial," "Victorian," and "Modern" (or is it "Contemporary"?) are imprecise terms. I also hope this guide helps the reader sort out the myriad styles that have enjoyed popularity throughout our history. Through an understanding of earlier styles, we develop insights into the architecture of our own era. Not only is it fun, but the study of architecture also nurtures a critical sense and allows us to make considered and informed judgments of what is being built today. We cannot legislate good taste, but we can hope to understand what's wrong with so much of our new building and perhaps do something about it.

The text is divided into chronological periods. An introductory historical overview precedes a concise commentary on each style. But before reading on I strongly urge the reader to review the Glossary. There are many architectural terms that may be unfamiliar; not knowing them will limit the value of this guide.

J.M.B.

The art of a civilization, rightly interpreted, is a very precise reflection of the society which produced it....In architecture, an art tied to practical purposes and executed always within severe practical limits, this dialectical law is more marked than in any other art.

—R. Furneaux Jordan, *a concise history of Western Architecture,* 1984

INTRODUCTION

America is a country of immigrants. The early settlers brought with them building techniques from their respective homelands and house types that matched those left behind. The different social conditions, as well as climate and terrain, however, influenced the development of American houses that were distinct from their European prototypes. It is important to remember that our houses have been shaped by their architectural forebears as much as we as individuals are shaped by our genetic and cultural backgrounds.

Just as the predominant ethnic group in America from the 1600s throughout most of the nineteenth century was British in origin, so was our architecture. We declared our independence from Britain in 1776, but culturally we remained closely tied to English architectural fashions. Even Jefferson's Neoclassicism and the Greek Revival of the 1820s and 1830s followed trends set in the mother country.

In the preface to his extraordinarily popular *Victorian Cottage Residences*, first published in 1842, Andrew Jackson Downing observed: "The very great interest now beginning to manifest itself in rural improvements of every kind, leads us to believe and to hope, that at no distant day our country residences may rival the 'cottage homes of England,' so universally and so justly admired." Downing was an extremely popular and widely read proponent of country houses. His books sold thousands of copies during the 1840s and 1850s and represented a prevalent attitude in this country. In his preface to the 1980 Dover edition, Adolf K. Placzek said that *Victorian Cottage Residences* was "one of the most widely used books in American architectural literature." No history of the American house in the nineteenth century can be separated from the English architecture of the Victorian era. (Our use of the British term "Victorian" is revealing.)

At their best our houses were simpler—not just smaller, which was generally true—and less pretentious than those in England. The principal differences developed from the greater extremes of our climate. The porch, or verandah, became a feature of most American houses because it helped to avert the heat of our summer sun and keep the houses cooler. The British had no need for the porch.

The flexibility of our floor plans was another important difference. Even in the 1820s we used recessed pocket doors to open a dining room and parlor into one large space in warm weather or for enter-

View from driveway

*A Shingle style house
designed by Walter Cook, 1887*

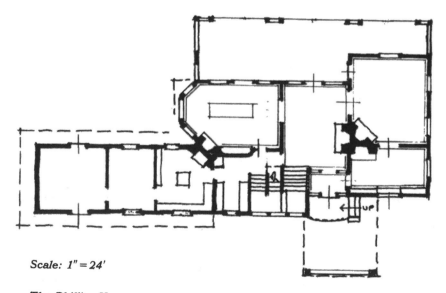

Scale: 1" = 24'

*The Phillips House
Bellport, Long Island, New York, 1887
        measured before demolition in 1960 by John Milnes Baker*

taining. The cozier spaces could be heated more easily with fire-places or the new parlor stoves. Central heating in the form of central warm-air furnaces was used here earlier than in Britain and it worked more effectively with an open floor plan. While central heating was not a concern in the design of large summer "cottages" built by the wealthy after the Civil War, the plans of the Shingle style houses often flowed in one continuous space from hall to parlor to dining room. The British tended to have more rooms allocated for specific uses. It is interesting to note that the the openness of our floor plans seemed to grow in direct proportion to our confidence as a nation.

By the turn of the century our houses were studied in European publications and it no longer took a generation for a European innovation to become popular here. *The Architectural Record* was available to British architects after 1891 and, significantly, Frank Lloyd Wright's (1867–1959) first retrospective was published in Germany by the Wasmuth Press in 1910. This folio had consider-able influence on architects abroad—particularly in Germany and Holland—and practically no influence on architects in America. From the end of the first decade of the twentieth century, America's self-confidence seemed to waver and our architecture reflected a taste for nostaligic revival of our own colonial styles as well as historical styles from abroad. Neoclassicism never really dies and continues to resurge with varying degrees of proficiency in each generation.

Richard Morris Hunt (1827–1895) was the first American to study at the Ecole des Beaux-Arts, a bastion of classical design in Paris. He returned to this country in 1855 and France became an increasingly important source of architectural inspiration. An in-creasing number of Americans studied in Paris in the years following the Civil War. Classicism won the day at the Columbian Exposition in Chicago (Chicago's world's fair) in 1893, and the Beaux-Arts style emerged in all its glory. Hunt's Beaux-Arts master plan gave a cohesive order to the exhibition buildings. Except for Louis Sul-livan's Transportation Building, virtually all the structures followed classical designs and had a tremendous influence on the Neoclassical revival which followed the fair. The innovative solutions to the new high-rise buildings in Chicago and the suburban houses by Wright and his fellow proponents of the Prairie School were eventually challenged by the revivalist movement after 1910.

*House near Utrecht, Holland
by Robert van't Hoff, 1916*

*Proposed design for
Harold F. McCormick, near Chicago
by Frank Lloyd Wright, 1907*

*Villa Turicum
Harold F. McCormick House,
by Charles A. Platt, 1908*

*Lovell Beach House,
Los Angeles, California
by R. M. Schindler, 1922–1926*

Wright's grandly conceived design for Harold F. McCormick over-looking Lake Michigan was ultimately rejected by the client and a more acceptable eastern architect was retained. Charles A. Platt (1861–1933) designed a perfectly mannered Italian pallazzo for the McCormicks, and the Prairie School lost its chance for social endorsement by the monied establishment.

Most houses built in the period from 1910 through the crash of 1929 tended to be reminiscent in style. This creative lull lasted until the Great Depression of the 1930s. It is interesting to note that Wright's career was in eclipse during this same period. He spent the years around the First World War in Japan creating the Imperial Hotel in Tokyo. The few houses that he did during the twenties were for strong-willed eccentric clients—mostly in southern California. (The Millard, Barnsdale, Freeman, and Storer houses were all in greater Los Angeles.)

The main innovative forces at work during this lull were significant but not widespread. Irving Gill and R. M. Schindler's work in California, for example, anticipated the Modern movement in isolation. While Cass Gilbert tried to negate the efforts of the Chicago School's search for an appropriate, inherent expression for the skyscraper by reverting to the Gothic style for his Woolworth Tower completed in 1913, Bernard Maybeck's funky Christian Science church in California and Wright's Unitarian Church in Oak Park, Illinois, were the last fresh efforts in church design for another generation. Spirited and competent but somehow soulless, the neo-Gothic churches of Ralph Cram and Bertram Goodhue (for example, St. John the Divine in 1921) and James Gamble Rogers's Harkness Tower at Yale (1931) seem self-conscious and forced in their settings.

Walter L. Dodge House,
Hollywood, California
by Irving Gill, 1916

There were many competent architects who responded to the more conventional or traditional tastes of the successful business men of the day. As derivative as much of their work was these talented and inventive architects designed beautifully scaled, livable houses. Harrie T. Lindeberg, Delano & Aldrich, Mellor, Meigs & Howe, and W. L. Bottomley were all outstanding in their field.

The House & Garden movement began in the early years of this century. The notion of an ideal life in the country—a life involving sports, animals, and growing one's fruits and vegetables—was new, modern, and very American. The architects who served these clients performed as much of a service for society as did those who embraced the minimalist aesthetic of the Modern school after 1929.

Red Gate
Seth Thomas House, New Vernon, New Jersey
by Harrie T. Lindeberg, 1926

Robert T. McCracken House, West Mt. Airy, Pennsylvania
by Mellor Meigs & Howe, 1920

In the 1930s the Modern movement became firmly established among the mainstream architects. Wright once again appeared on the scene with his famous Fallingwater and his first of what he called his "Usonian" houses for the Jacobs family near Madison, Wisconsin. The development of the American house during the past half-century is a fascinating drama; but first let us go back to the beginning and a look at the early efforts of the colonial period.

Herbert Jacob's House, Madison, Wisconsin, 1937

Fallingwater
Edgar J. Kauffman House
Bear Run, Pennsylvania
by Frank Lloyd Wright, 1936
I have always felt that Fallingwater, Frank Lloyd Wright's only great
house using the characteristic elements of the International style, was
his comment to the Internationalists: "If that's what you want, boys, I'll
show you how it should be done!" The flat roofs, reinforced concerete
with bold cantilevers, industrial windows, all part of the Modern
vocabulary, were used by Wright without compromising his own sense of
site and place—his sense of space.

It is altogether unlikely that such words as architecture *and* style *were even in the vocabularies of the early settlers, much less in common usage.*

— Marshall B. Davidson, *The American Heritage History of Notable American Houses*, 1971

1. EARLY COLONIAL   1600–1715

"Colonial," without "Spanish," "French," or "Dutch" to modify the term, generally means English Colonial. The first English settlements were established at Jamestown, Virginia, in 1607 and in Plymouth, Massachusetts, in 1620 when the Pilgrims arrived on the *Mayflower.* By the end of the turbulent years of the English Civil War and Oliver Cromwell's Commonwealth in 1660 (the year King Charles II was restored to the throne), thousands of settlers left England for the New World. Of a total population in 1657 of barely 200,000, over ninety percent came from England, approximately six percent from Holland, and the rest from all other countries combined.* The Massachusetts Bay Colony drew largely from East Anglia—Suffolk, Norfolk, Cambridgeshire, and Essex—and the South drew more from the southern and western counties. Settlers came for diverse reasons—many for religious freedom, some as bonded servants, and most for economic gain.

The houses built in British North America in both the North and the South during the seventeenth century were late medieval structures. More accurately, they were late Tudor and Jacobean buildings: asymmetrical, informal designs with steeply pitched roofs and gabled ends. The builders used the same construction techniques as were used in the farmsteads and modest village houses they had left behind.

It may be helpful to remember that Queen Elizabeth I, the last of the Tudor line, died in 1603, and James Stuart, King James VI of Scotland, became James I of England. (His reign was known as the Jacobean period.) Charles I followed in 1625 but was arrested in 1642 and executed in 1649. The Stuart line continued after Cromwell's Commonwealth with the restoration of Charles II to the throne in 1660; it lasted until 1714 when Queen Anne died and was succeeded by George I, the first Hanoverian.

In England, the seventeenth century saw the beginning of the English Renaissance in Inigo Jones's buildings in 1620, the Commonwealth under Oliver Cromwell from 1649 until 1660 when the royal court sought refuge in Holland, and the flourishing of what was sometimes called the "Wrenaissance" after the incredibly prolific Sir

*Colkert, Meredith B., Jr., *Founders of Early American Families—Emigrants from Europe 1607–1657* (Cleveland, OH: The Founders and Patriots of America, 1985), p. xxv.

Christopher Wren (1632–1723) in the late Stuart period. Dutch influence was strong, and we should not forget that William of Orange ousted James II in 1688. William ruled England (with his wife Mary Stuart as William and Mary and after her death as William III) until he died in 1702.

When the Pilgrims landed at Plymouth in 1620, Inigo Jones's (1573–1652) Banqueting Hall in London was almost completed and his house for the queen in Greenwich was still under construction (see page 34). These were the first Renaissance buildings in England, but they had no more impact on the early colonial houses in America than the White House had on the California bungalow.

When Henry VIII broke with Rome in 1542 he dissolved the monasteries. Their vast properties were subdivided into substantial estates. Manor houses and tenant farmsteads went up in a surge of building. Though large timber-framed houses were still built in the forested counties of Warwickshire, Lancashire, and Cheshire, brick became the most popular building material. Imported from Holland, it was first used in East Anglia, and the Dutch soon introduced brickmaking there in the sixteenth century. Hampton Court near London and Compton Wynyates in Warwickshire are both enormous Tudor houses built of brick.

Coal was first used extensively for heat in the Tudor period. Fireplaces with projecting chimney stacks were developed as a way to exhaust the oily smoke above the roof. In earlier days wood fires were simply built on the floor of the great hall and the smoke allowed to escape through vents at the top of the double-storied space. Chimney stacks became an important decorative feature of the late Tudor house and remained a key element in the early colonial houses built here.

Windows were also expressive features in the Tudor and Jacobean period. Large stone or wooden frames were built with mullions separating the openings. (The wooden glazing bars in the sash window introduced from Holland in the late seventeenth century are called muntins. They are often mistakenly called mullions which are the structural posts between windows.) Operating sash were hinged casements. Panes were small and held together by a lead framework such as you might see in a stained-glass church window today. The diamond-paned, leaded-glass casement window 'was incorporated into our early houses. Glass had to be brought from England and was very expensive; as a result, it occupied only a small percentage of the exterior walls. Except for restorations, original leaded windows were replaced with double-hung, wooden sash windows in the early eighteenth century. Exterior louvered blinds (incorrectly called shutters today) were not used in England and were never a feature of the early colonial house here. Shutters (at first solid boarding and later paneled) were used for security but were not featured as a decorative element or as a climate-control device.

Most early colonial survivors are restorations. Several still exist and are open to the public. In a day's drive around Boston, one can visit the towns of Ipswich, Salem, and the Ironworks at Saugus, Massachusetts. Early houses in the South are fewer and more spread out, but the Thoroughgood House near Norfolk, Virginia, and Bacon's Castle in Surry County, Virginia, are excellent examples.

Saugus Ironmaster's House,
Saugus, Massachusetts, c. 1680

Thoroughgood House, Norfolk, Virginia, c. 1650

EARLY NEW ENGLAND COLONIAL   1640–1715

The half-timbered houses of early New England were covered with a beveled siding of wooden clapboards. Called weatherboarding in England, it was relatively rare in the northern counties because wood was increasingly expensive. The bountiful New England forests, however, made wooden siding an obvious choice here and provided the essential element of our early colonial houses that has continued to this day. As in England, front doors were vertical boards attached to an inner layer of horizontal boards; the outer surface often had hand-wrought nails with their exposed heads forming a decorative pattern—a subtle form of conspicuous consumption. The more nails the more extravagance.

The steeply pitched roofs of the English thatched-roof cottage were constructed here in the same manner, but thatch was quickly replaced by split shingles, or "shakes," which fared better in our severe winters. Window glass was usually set in diamond-shaped patterns of leaded panes. Decorative embellishments were generally subtle and understated; there were very few exceptions. One was the massive central chimneys of stone or brick with their clustered flues; another was the occasional "drop" or pendant under the jetted overhang of the second floor. The houses were seldom painted but were simply oiled or left to weather.

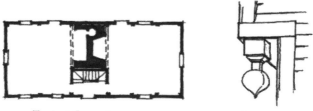

Typical floor plan   *Drop*

By the end of the seventeenth century some buildings were being built here in the classical Renaissance style. The Christopher Wren building at the College of William and Mary in Williamsburg, Virginia, was started in 1695 and completed in 1702. Although it is usually called Georgian, I have always had trouble using that term for a building completed several years before the first George came to the English throne. Stuart or even Restoration would be more appropriate terms.

EARLY NEW ENGLAND COLONIAL 1640–1715

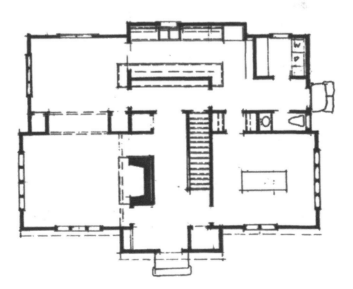

EARLY SOUTHERN COLONIAL   1640–1715

The colonies of Virginia and Maryland were settled in the early seventeenth century, and the houses were essentially transplanted English structures. Brick made from the southern clay was the common building material for substantial buildings.

The cross-gabled plan was typical of these early colonial houses and diamond-paned, leaded windows were the norm. In contrast to the central chimneys of New England, which retained the heat in the cold climate, southern houses placed the chimneys at the gable ends and usually separated the upper chimney stack from the building by several inches. Coals were kept burning at all times, even in summer.

Some early houses, Bacon's Castle in Virginia for example, had parapeted gable ends with the Flemish or Dutch gables characteristic of East Anglia—an area with close ties to Holland in the early 1600s. Chimneys were elaborate compositions with each flue stack separated from the others and often fluted with decorative motifs following the Tudor precedent.

Though wood did not fare well in the hot and humid climate of the South, frame houses were also built. They tended to be one-story structures with raised basements. They had clapboard siding and the roofs were shingled.

What are often mistakenly called Southern Colonial—columned temples evoking images of Tara in the movie version of *Gone with the Wind*—in fact were post–Revolutionary War buildings of the antebellum days and were typically Greek Revival in style (see page 64).

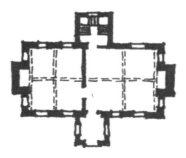

Typical "hall and parlor" plan

Chimney detail,
Bacon's Castle, Surry County, Virginia

EARLY SOUTHERN COLONIAL 1640–1715

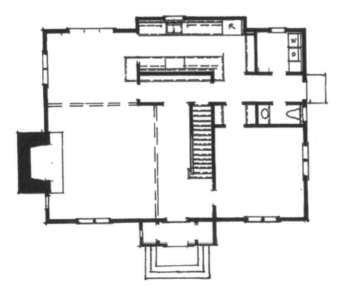

Emigrants to the New World, like their middle and lower class countrymen who stayed at home, neglected matters of style and fashion in favor of more elementary, practical, and traditional construction.

—Marshall B. Davidson, *The American Heritage History of Notable American Houses,* 1971

2. COLONIAL   1600–1780

ENGLISH   1700–1780

Toward the end of the seventeenth century many changes occurred in the appearance of our colonial houses. They no longer had an old-world medieval look. Double-hung windows (often called "sash windows") had recently been introduced into England from Holland and soon found their way here. They were used almost exclusively by 1715. The panes were small, about 6 inches by 8 inches with 1-inch-thick muntins. Older houses were usually retrofitted with the new windows and the colonial house assumed a very different look from its earlier period.

Roofs became less steep—about 38 degrees instead of 50 degrees or more—and chimneys no longer had the clustered mass of their late-medieval prototypes. They were still large and centrally located in New England until well into the eighteenth century at which time the floor plan acquired a central hallway and chimneys were moved to either side of the house.

The original seventeenth-century rectangular "hall and parlor" layout was usually enlarged with the addition of a lean-to shed at the back creating the familiar saltbox shape. By the turn of the century saltboxes had become so standard that they were built with the long sloping roof as a deliberate element.

Plan
Typical
Saltbox

Typical
Center hall
Colonial

The equally familiar Cape Cod cottage evolved (not just on Cape Cod) as a one-story or one-and-a-half-story house. Originally these houses were built without dormers. Shingle siding was common, although clapboard siding continued to be used. Incidentally, these houses were rarely painted white before the nineteenth century when the Greek Revival craze swept the country.

What makes these houses Colonial, as opposed to Georgian, is their lack of fancy ornamentation. Embellishments of eaves, window heads, and door surrounds with even vestiges of classical details would make them Georgian or Georgian Colonial.

COLONIAL HOUSES

Cape Cod Cottage

New England Saltbox

Double pile house—
Two rooms deep on both floors

Southern house

ENGLISH

Urban house

Urban row house

DUTCH

Rural farm house

DUTCH   1625–1800

New Netherland was founded in 1625. It extended from the Delaware River to what roughly corresponds to the New York/New England border. New Amsterdam and Fort Orange were renamed New York and Albany after the English seized the colony in 1664. (Although the Dutch regained New Netherland, they traded it for what is now Surinam in a 1674 treaty.)

The Dutch tradition placed the gabled end of their houses toward the street where it provided access to storage in the attic. Holland had no forests by the sixteenth century and brick was their principal building material. It was also used extensively in New Netherland. The bricks were often brought in ships' holds as ballast. Windows were casements in the early houses, but double-hung sash windows became the norm after 1715. Parapeted brick gables were the standard for the attached urban rowhouse. What has become identified as Dutch Colonial was supposedly derived from the Flemish farmhouse with its flared gambrel roof, but even this theory is open to debate.

The Dutch effectively won their independence from Spain by 1609 (the same year that Henry Hudson claimed the river that bears his name for the Dutch West India Company). Though nominally a monarchy, Holland was the first nation to be ruled by burghers in the form of the Estates General. Holland was essentially a mercantile country and trade was the source of wealth rather than the English notion of landed estates. They were a tolerant people and Holland became a refuge for Huguenots from France, Pilgrims from England, and Jews from Spain. The Dutch were never comfortable with the strict dictums of Renaissance architecture, which to them was associated with an authoritarian form of government and an aristocratic social order. Comfort, privacy, and a sense of domesticity were ideas developed by the Dutch in this era.* Dutch building had a great influence on English architecture in the early seventeenth century. Flemish or Dutch gables were popular Jacobean features in England, as were brick, double-hung sash windows, and solid shutters.

---

*See Rybczynski, Witold, *Home, A Short History of an Idea* (New York: Viking, 1986).

SPANISH   1600s–1840s

Spain came to the New World to find riches and to save souls. The Spanish had a mission of the sword as well as a mission of the cross. They founded missions throughout what is now our Southwest as well as Florida and California. Their churches were often elaborate architectural achievements, particularly in Texas and Arizona.

Ponce de León first attempted to found a colony in Florida at St. Augustine in 1513 but it failed. The colony founded at Tampa, however, succeeded in 1528. (This was one hundred years before the Massachusetts Bay Colony.) Missions proliferated throughout the Spanish territory during the eighteenth century. The architecture varied from crude huts to elaborate Baroque churches with intricate detail. The oldest house in America built by Europeans was the Governor's Palace erected in Sante Fe, New Mexico, in 1609. It was the prototype for the Pueblo style (see pages 128–29). There are three other residential legacies from the Spanish era. The Spanish Mission churches inspired the Spanish Mission style (see pages 126–27), the one-story California *ranchos* built after 1821 sired our ranch houses (see page 148), and the blending of the New England colonial and the Spanish *casa* resulted in the Monterey style (see pages 132–33).

Governor's Palace, Santa Fe, New Mexico, 1609–1614

FRENCH   1700–1825

In the mid-eighteenth century the French colonial territory extended from the Alleghenies to the Rocky Mountains and from Labrador and Hudson's Bay to the Gulf of Mexico. France controlled virtually all of the Great Lakes and the entire Mississippi River. Considering the size of the French domain, it is surprising that so little architecture of the colonial days has survived. The French built forts and trading posts but not new towns. There are no early surviving buildings in Detroit or St. Louis, and New Orleans was practically destroyed by fires before 1800. With the exception of the galleried plantation house, French colonial architecture had almost no impact on subsequent house styles. Remember that the British prevailed in the French and Indian Wars which ended in 1763, and Jefferson made the Louisiana Purchase from the French in 1803.

Early seventeenth-century French-style houses were generally rectangular in plan and had no interior hallways. They had steeply pitched hip roofs. Sometimes a *gallerie* or verandah was included under the main roof or was sheltered by a roof with a shallower pitch. In damp locations the main floor was elevated several feet above grade. In the larger plantation houses in Louisiana this basement became an entire story and contained storage and utility space. Most of these survivors had French doors and galleries. The mid-nineteenth-century cast-iron balconies seen in New Orleans were chronologically Victorian and had no precedent in France. The gallery reappeared about 1830 as a feature of the Greek Revival house in the antebellum days of the "New South."

Parlange, Pointe Coupee Parish, Louisiana, 1750

. . . the Georgian, with its formal symmetry and finer materials and delicately executed ornament, was the expression of a wealthy and polite society.

—Hugh Morrison, *Early American Architecture,* 1952

3. GEORGIAN   1715–1780

When the Great Fire of London consumed the city in 1666, Sir Christopher Wren (1632–1723) was the architect chosen to rebuild it. The conflagration virtually put an end to the medieval city, and the classical forms of the Renaissance predominated in its reconstruction.

With the restoration of Charles II to the English throne in 1660 the Renaissance style flourished. The houses built in this era were generally restrained, dignified, and refined classical buildings which served as the prototypes for the best of the Georgian architecture in the American colonies.

Queen Anne was the last of the Stuart monarchs. She died in 1714 and was succeeded by George I—the beginning of the Georgian era. With the exception of a few lavish Baroque essays built during her reign, like Sir John Vanbrugh's Blenheim Palace and Nicholas Hawksmoor's Castle Howard, most Queen Anne houses were relatively modest. It was the character of these late Stuart houses that set the tone of the American Colonial Georgian period.

Throughout our Colonial Georgian era, very little of the the actual English Georgian architecture even reached North America until after the Revolution. Our Federal and Neoclassical architecture then borrowed from the English Georgian styles of the mid-eighteenth century.

Two important influences shaped the character of English residential architecture of our Georgian period. One was the Dutch architecture of the late seventeenth century with its use of brick and contrasting sandstone, hipped roofs, and domestic scale. The other was the Palladian movement. Renaissance classicism bloomed under Wren but the self-conscious and rigid Palladianism evolved during the reign of George I. The English translation of Andrea Palladio's *Four Books of Architecture* and the first part of Colen Campbell's *Vitruvius Britannicus*, an elaborate treatise with Palladian designs recommended for Britain, were published in 1715. Both books had a formidable influence on residential architecture.

To understand Georgian architecture one must know something about Andrea Palladio (1518–1580), who was one of the most influential architects of all time. A native of Vicenza, his country houses inland from Venice were unlike anything that had been built before. They inspired generations of architects, dilettantes, and scholars.

STUART ARCHITECTURE

Queen's House, Greenwich, England, by Inigo Jones, begun 1617

Squerryes Court,
Westerham, Kent, c. 1680

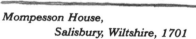

Mompesson House,
Salisbury, Wiltshire, 1701

Belton House, near Grantham, Lincolnshire, 1684–1688

His innovations became gospel for British architects from Inigo Jones and Sir Christopher Wren in the seventeenth century throughout the Georgian era of the eighteenth century. His influence was felt in the American colonies and is still in evidence today even if in vestigial form.

AMERICAN GEORGIAN
American Georgian houses built after 1715 were based on the Stuart architecture of late seventeenth-century England.

Westover,
near Charles City, Virginia, 1734

Hunter House,
Newport, Rhode Island, c. 1746

Wentworth-Gardner House,
Portsmouth, New Hampshire, 1760

Corbit House,
Odessa, Delaware, 1772–1774

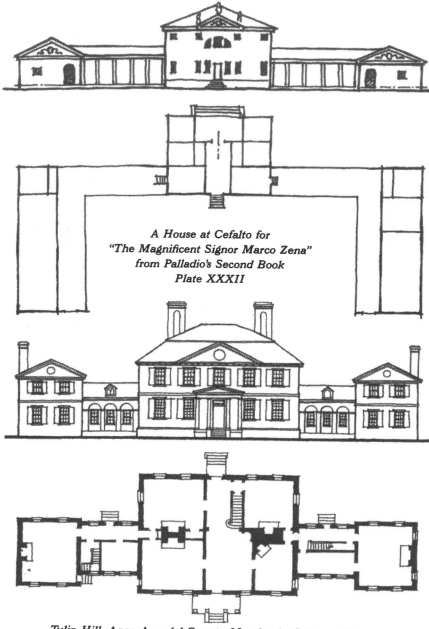

*A House at Cefalto for
"The Magnificent Signor Marco Zena"
from Palladio's Second Book
Plate XXXII*

Tulip Hill, Anne Arundel County, Maryland, 1745–c. 1785

By the mid-sixteenth century, Venice had become an immensely wealthy independent city-state. The new humanistic doctrine fostered an intellectual community with a cultured upper class that was distinctly separate from Rome. The Venetians even developed an empathy with the Protestantism that was emerging in northern Europe. It was in this milieu that Palladio found an outlet for his talents.

What was so special about Palladio and why was he different from other Renaissance architects? The inventor of a new kind of country house—one that became the prototype for the eighteenth-century English estates and the plantation houses of the American South— he codified a personal adaptation of the ancient classical orders and developed a system of harmonic proportions for his spaces. His sophisticated farmhouses for an educated agrarian class were rural structures that incorporated the functional components of a working farm into ordered and controlled compositions. Even the attic space of many of his houses was used to store hay! The now-familiar five-part composition—central block with symmetrical dependencies connected by hyphens—was Palladio's innovation and was one attribute of his work that was widely imitated by his followers.

The other two principal features that characterize Palladio's work were his use of the central pedimented portico to emphasize the importance of the entrance facade and the reintroduction of the dome in a domestic building. Both features had long been associated with religious buildings and were as strange as a church steeple would be on a suburban house today. He incorporated these elements into his designs to infuse his houses with a sense of "grandeur" and "magnificence" (two of his favorite words). He felt obliged to justify the use of both the pediment and the dome by explaining in his *Four Books of Architecture* that they were originally derived from domestic structures (hence the word *domus*) and were therefore a legitimate use of the forms.

Palladio also used a mundane finish material on these grand houses: plain stucco or plaster instead of cut stone. The plain surfaces were painted warm earthy tones which infused them with a richness of light and color that was more akin to the vernacular architecture of Italy than to the pallazzos of Rome and Florence. These were inexpensive materials, and their simplicity was a subtle counterpoint to the richness of his details.

It is interesting that a handful of country villa/farmhouses and a single anomalous belvedere, the Villa Capra (Villa Rotunda) near Venice, would launch Palladio's name into western residential architecture. His word was spread with almost evangelical flame by his English proponents in the eighteenth century. Many of his admirers had traveled to Italy and seen his work. His four-volume treatise on architecture included many of his own designs as well as measured drawings of ancient Roman buildings. As a writer he was a first-rate public relations expert and it was his books, as much as his actual buildings, that lead to his great renown. Lord Burlington (1694–1753) was his single most important promoter in Britain in concert with Colen Campbell (d. 1729). Both built houses based on the Villa Rotunda.

Villa Emo, Fanzolo, Italy, by Palladio, 1559

Villa Capra (Villa Rotunda),
Vicenza, Italy,
by Palladio, 1556–1570

Mereworth Castle, Kent,   *Chiswick,*
by Colen Campbell, 1723   Lord Burlington's House, Middlesex, 1720s

Before examining the various styles that derive from classical prototypes, I want to focus on one detail that is often constructed incorrectly—always to the detriment of classical design. The difference is not generally understood or appreciated.

Throughout the eighteenth and nineteenth centuries there were pattern books that provided builders with classical details based on accurate, measured drawings of actual classical buildings. The two drawings below show the right and the wrong way to construct the cornice. If one is going to use the details, it might as well be done correctly. Asher Benjamin stated, though admittedly not all that clearly, in his 1827 edition of *The American Builder's Companion*, "It is to be observed, that the cymarecta and fillet above it, of the cornice, are always omitted in the horizontal one of the pediment; that part of the profile being directed upward to finish the inclined cornices." Though somewhat verbose, the author is specific in his instruction that the S-shaped crown molding, the cymarecta, caps the top of the pediment and is not returned on the horizontal corona.

CORNICE DETAILS

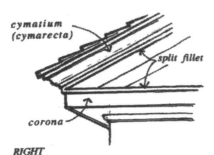

This is the only place the crown molding should be positioned. Note that the crown molding— the cymarecta—follows up the rake above the upper part of the "split" or "hinged" fillet and not on the lower part just above the horizontal corona.

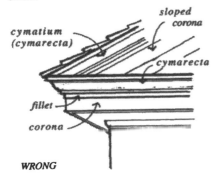

Though you often you see this detail, it is flat and uninteresting when compared to the correct classical standard. It places the emphasis on the horizontal portion of the pediment rather than on the rake.

CLASSICAL ORDERS

*There are five Renaissance orders.
The Composite order, however, is
extremely rare and is quite similar in
proportion and scale to
the Corinthian.*

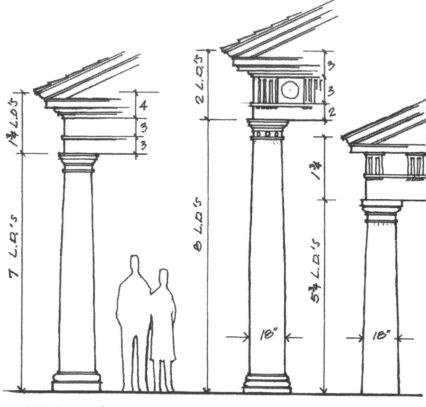

All L.D.s = 18"   Scale: ¼" = 1'-0"   **Greek Doric**

TUSCAN *8¾ Lower Diameters*   **ROMAN DORIC** *10 L.D.s*

The component parts of the classical orders are all proportioned to the
diameter of the lower part of the column. Columns curve inward for the
upper two-thirds of their height. (All the orders shown here have the
same lower diameter of 18 inches.) (See page 171)

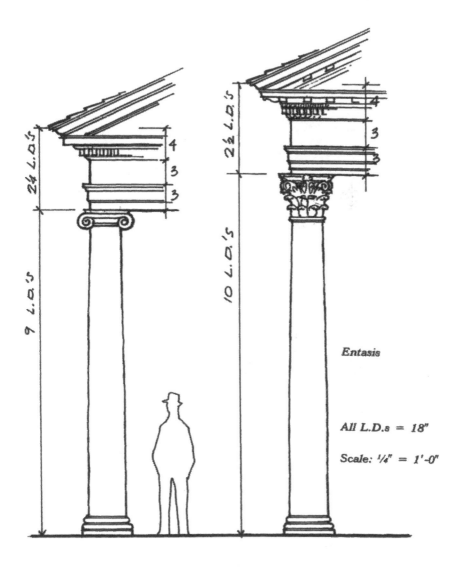

Entasis

All L.D.s = 18"

Scale: ¼" = 1'-0"

IONIC *11¼ Lower Diameters*   **CORINTHIAN** *12½ L.D.s*

The columns vary from seven to ten L.D.s in height. The entablatures are one-quarter the height of the column, and the divisions of the architrave, frieze, and cornice are governed by strict rules. The Greek Doric order was 7½ L.D.s and the column only 5¾ and had no base.

GEORGIAN—New England   1715–1780

Whether built in the North, the South, or the Middle Atlantic colonies of Delaware, Pennsylvania, or New York, the same simple formality epitomized this new popular style. Symmetry, aligned windows, and accepted conventions based on Renaissance precedent for all the basic component parts of the house characterize the American Georgian style. The proliferation of English pattern books served to ensure a unanimity or consistency of design throughout the colonies. There were regional differences based on available materials, cultural patterns, and social attitudes, but the variations were all on a basic theme.

Roofs were either gambrel, gabled, or hipped. The gambrel was much more common in New England than in the other regions. The illustration shows the gambrel roof on a house one could find in Portsmouth, New Hampshire, Newport, Rhode Island, or up the Connecticut River Valley.

The New England Georgian house of the mid-eighteenth century usually had a distinctive paneled door accentuated by classical pilasters and capped by a well-proportioned, pedimented entablature. A transom light, either rectangular or half-round, was common, but neither side lights nor elliptical fanlights appeared until after the Revolution.

Windows were surrounded by molded architraves and capped with classical crown moldings or cornices. The eaves, by definition, had classical cornices often with modillions on the soffits. The upper windows were usually set just below the eaves and were the same size as the lower windows. Divided lights were set in 1-inch-thick muntins and were 6 inches by 8 inches or 8 inches by 10 inches at the largest. Glass was still imported and still very dear. After 1750 the balustrade was introduced and was generally set high on the roof. Neither louvered blinds nor shutters were a feature of the New England Georgian house. Louvered blinds were introduced late in the eighteenth century and probably came from the South.

Georgian houses generally did not have covered porches at the front door. There might be pilasters framing the doorway with an entablature above projecting a few inches from the face of the wall, but no roof supported by columns. Whenever an entry porch appears on a Georgian house it was probably added after the Revolutionary War.

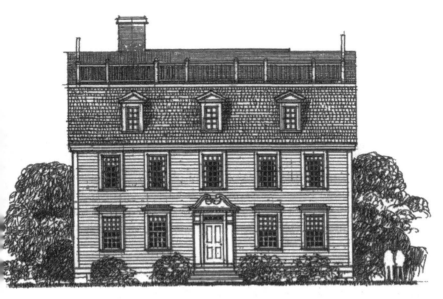

GEORGIAN—New England 1715–1780

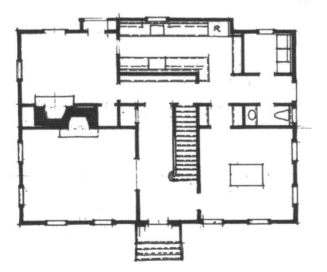

GEORGIAN—The Middle Atlantic   1715–1780

Stone was the most common building material in Pennsylvania and the Delaware Valley. Unlike New England, lime was readily available and the settlers—who came mostly from the midlands of England—were accustomed to masonry construction. Philadelphia was by far the largest city in the colonies at that time and certainly had the finest architecture. Though he never actually settled there himself, William Penn brought architect/builders with him to his new colony. Most of the settlers were Quakers and came from the Penine moorlands.

Somewhat heavier moldings and details were seen on these buildings than in the other colonies—perhaps to reflect the more massive quality of the stone. The fully pedimented gable with its horizontal corona returned across the gabled ends. The cornice was often highly decorated with modillions and dentil work.

Though paneled shutters were introduced in the colonial period, louvered blinds came in quite late and were often seen just on the upper floor. Even today around Philadelphia you will see white shutters on the lower story and dark-green louvered blinds above.

A distinctive feature of the Pennsylvania house was the "pent"—an appended roof that was secured or hung from the wall above without brackets or posts to support it. Called a "pentice" in England, it was common in the midlands. Sometimes the pent extended all the way across the face of the building and, as shown in the illustration, occasionally with a pedimented portion that emphasized the front doors and diverted the rain from the porch below.

The double-hung windows, typical of all Colonial Georgian houses, tended to be "6 over 6" (that is, 6 panes in the upper sash and 6 panes below), 6 over 9, or 9 over 12 with 1-inch-thick muntins. Generally the glass size was still fairly small—6 inches by 8 inches or only slightly larger.

House with pent

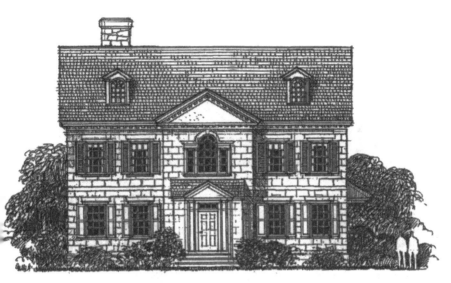

GEORGIAN—The Middle Atlantic 1715–1780

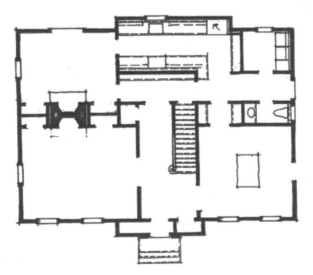

GEORGIAN — The South   1715–1780

Brick was by far the most common building material in the southern colonies for large houses, usually laid in Flemish bond (alternating headers and stretchers). The hip roof, while sometimes used further north, predominated in the southern colonies. The influence of the restrained late-Stuart style of residential architecture was at its peak in the plantation houses of the Virginia tidewater prior to the Revolution.

As in the English prototype, window panes were small, the muntins at least 1-inch thick, and the exterior casings rather narrow. The major decorative elements were featured at the eaves in the form of classical cornice detail often enriched with modillions and occasionally a pedimented doorway with a well-proportioned transom light. Semi-circular transoms were common as were rectangular ones. Remember that sidelights and elliptical fanlights were not used in any of the colonies until after the Revolution. The Brewton House in Charleston, South Carolina, built between 1765 and 1769, is "the only undoubtedly authentic example of this motive in a pre-Revolutionary house."*

The best examples of the style can be seen in Virginia. The Wythe House at Williamsburg (1755) is an excellent example. Also Stratford, Carter's Grove, and Westover, all built between 1725 and 1753. Mount Airy, finished in 1762, was copied from English architect James Gibbs's *Book of Architecture* and is pure Palladian.

*Mount Airy,
Warsaw, Virginia, c. 1762*

Although most southern Colonial Georgian houses were brick, Mount Vernon is the most notable exception. It was timberframe with wooden siding. But even there, when Washington remodeled the house in 1757, he not only simulated masonry by incising the boards to look like stone blocks, but he actually textured the siding with a paint mixed with sand (see page 52).

*Morrison, Hugh, *Early American Architecture* (New York: Oxford University Press, 1952; Dover, 1987), p. 416.

GEORGIAN—The South 1715–1780

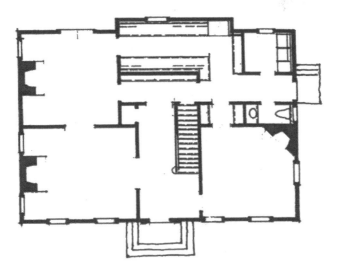

More so than ever in the colonial period, buildings were now not only frameworks in which to live and work; they were also provocative projections of what Americans wanted to be.

—David P. Handlin, *American Architecture*, 1985

4. THE YOUNG REPUBLIC   1780–1820

The Treaty of Paris in 1783, seven years after our Declaration of Independence, confirmed our nationhood but not our sense of nationality. There were too many disparate forces to be merged to expect a spontaneous social order that encompassed all our differences. Benjamin Franklin admonished at the time, "Say, rather, the War of the Revolution. The War of Independence is yet to be fought." Democracy was still a dubious and volatile experiment.

There was no White House and no capitol dome to symbolize our unity. Philadelphia, not Washington, was the nation's capital for over ten years. After a brief time in New York, the capital was located in Philadelphia from 1790 until 1801. William Penn's Quaker town had grown to be the largest city in the confederation—over 70,000 inhabitants and, next to London, the largest English-speaking city in the world. New York trailed by 10,000 and Boston had a mere 25,000 inhabitants. Strongly Tory during the Revolution, Philadelphia remained a patrician city and still felt comfortable with the late Georgian architecture of the mother country as did Boston, Newport, Salem, Charleston, and most other centers of commerce.

Not every colonist supported the Revolution—perhaps as many as a third of the population were loyalists even as late as 1800. When war broke out between England and France in 1793 there was a strong British sentiment among the Federalists. Jefferson's Republicans, more like the Democratic party of today, favored France. George Washington warned against our involvement in the quarrels of foreign nations in his farewell address in 1796. Our failure to heed his sagacious advice did much to polarize society in the years that followed, in a time when the former colonies needed cohesion.

This was also a time of financial crisis. The federal debt in 1790 was $54,000,000. On the other hand the government owned enormous amounts of land confiscated from the British Crown as well as individual loyalists' holdings. This land was made available to an increasing number of freeholders both in the former colonies and in the hinterland. The Northwest Ordinance of 1787 affirmed the equality of new states entering the union and was a great incentive to settlers who could move to the frontier with confidence that their rights would be protected. New states soon followed the original thirteen: Vermont in 1791, Kentucky in 1792, and Tennessee in 1796 were formed from federally owned territories or those sections where all disputed claims were withdrawn by the former colonies.

After the War of 1812, which Franklin might well have considered the real "War of Independence," America was well on its way to becoming a self-sustaining nation. The Louisiana Purchase in 1803 nurtured the shared ideal of a manifest destiny so much a part of our national psyche by mid-century. What about our architecture?

In the years before our independence the character of English Georgian architecture had begun to change. Archaeological discoveries at Herculaneum in 1719 and Pompeii in 1748 showed that the classical orders had much greater variety than Palladio or Vignola, another important architect who codified the classical orders, reported in the sixteenth century or than Vitruvius recorded in classical Rome. The Neoclassicism that was spurred by Thomas Jefferson drew not just from Palladio but also from the influential book *Antiquities of Athens* by Nicholas Revett and James Stuart, published in England in 1762. It is hard for us today to imagine that the use of one Ionic capital instead of another would be considered revolutionary. In fact, to a rigid Palladian, it was an extremely bold and unorthodox step.

This classicism of the early nineteenth century is often called Adamesque or the Adam style after Robert Adam (1728–1792) and his brothers who developed the style. They enjoyed the largest and most successful architectural practice in Britain from 1760 to 1780. With offices in London and Edinburgh, they were also developers in the way we use the term today. Although they drew from Palladio's work in their early years, their later work demonstrated a freer interpretation of the classical orders, extensive use of decorative panels, and, by American standards of the day, an excessively gaudy use of color and gilt in their interiors.

Typical Federal and Adam details

George Washington enlarged Mount Vernon between 1775 and 1777 in the latest fashion. The new dining/reception room was pure Adam (decorated much like Wedgewood china with Greek urns, sheaves of wheat, and garlands of flowers). Also at this time Washington added the two-story portico on the river elevation. Rather an anomaly, it is probably the single most recognized house in America. Undoubtedly few would recognize it in its original form, for it started life around 1735 as a typical one-and-a-half-story colonial farmhouse with a second story added in the 1750s. It took its final form in the Federal period (see illustration page 52).

The new freedom of the Federal period produced a lighter, more attenuated architecture which featured bowed windows, gracefully curved stairs, and tall 6 over 6 windows with delicate muntins only ¾-inch thick and large individual panes. Charles Bulfinch (1763–1844) of Boston, Samuel McIntyre (1757–1811) of Salem, Massachusetts, and William Thornton (1759–1828) of Washington were all proponents of this new and elegant expression of the late Renaissance ideal.

Thomas Jefferson sympathized with France in England's Napoleonic Wars (1799–1815) and looked to the continent for his architectural stimulation and prototypes for his interpretation of Neoclassicism. France had supported us in our fight against England and Jefferson was our minister to France from 1785 until the outbreak of their revolution in 1789. His Neoclassicism drew from the original sources—true Roman buildings such as the Maison Carrée in Nîmes—rather than work distilled by late eighteenth-century British architects.

Whatever the political predilection of the architect, Federal and Neoclassical houses shared many standards and infused their plans and details with numerous innovations. Closets, as we know them, appeared, along with butler's pantries and rooms with specific purposes. No longer were rooms invariably rectangular; elliptical, octagonal, and circular shapes were introduced as well as curved or bowed projections and octagonal bays. Service stairs and even indoor privies began to appear. Jefferson eliminated ceremonial stairways and even incorporated skylights into his designs.

By the end of the Federal period the classical idiom was recognized as an American way of building and set the pace for the Greek Revival of the next couple of generations. As settlers moved into the hinterlands, the Federal style had no time to take root before the

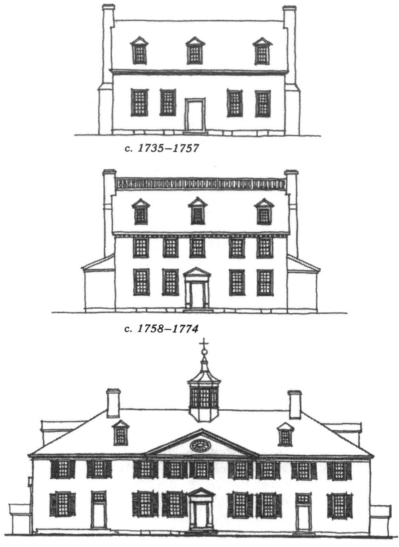

c. *1735–1757*

c. *1758–1774*

1775–1787

Mount Vernon was originally built about 1735 by George Washington's father as a typical unpretentious colonial farmhouse. It was enlarged and embellished with Georgian details in 1757–1758 and remodeled again during the Revolution. It took its final form by 1787.

popular mania for the Greek orders became established. Most Federal houses were built in towns founded before the Revolution.

Though Andrew Jackson won the most electoral votes in the 1824 election, the vote moved to the House of Representatives and he lost to John Quincy Adams. Four years later, however, Jackson won with a clear majority of the nation behind him and was the first "candidate of the common man." Jackson's Greek Revival house The Hermitage was a symbol of the new age.

The Hermitage,
Andrew Jackson's home, near Nashville, Tennessee, built in the 1830s

FEDERAL   1780–1820

In the early Federal period, the colonies found expression in a refined and elegant interpretation of the prescribed Georgian. William Hamilton's Woodlands just outside Philadelphia was among the first houses to be built in the new style. It was embellished with a two-story portico in the late 1780s.

The Woodlands,
Philadelphia, 1787–1789

Window glass was now made in the United States and was available in larger sizes. Three-story houses, with windows decreasing in height on the upper floors, became increasingly common. Three-quarter-inch glazing bars gave a new elegance to the Federal house and the divided lights were often 10 inches by 12 inches or even larger. Windows were elongated with the sills almost at the floor level. Elegant balustrades were set just above the eave line and the roof pitch was reduced to 4 in 12 and perceived as virtually flat. The Palladian window, popular during the Georgian period, became more delicate and was a common feature of the Federal house.

Charles Bulfinch returned to Boston from the London of the Adams brothers in 1786 and did much to alter Boston in the Federal period. The previous Georgian style deferred to the new influences from abroad.

Front doors with elliptical fanlight transoms and decorated side-lights became a feature of the Federal style. Wall surfaces were left plain. String or belt courses and occasional plaques with swags or sheaves of wheat might be the only decorative features. Considered elegant and rich by many admirers, the original Adam interiors in England were found by others to be garish and excessive in their gilded details and use of multicolored marble. The Adam style here generally showed more restraint and elegance in the understated playfulness of curved bays, oval rooms, and sweeping stairways. Some of the finest examples of the style can be seen in ports along the East Coast with strong ties to England.

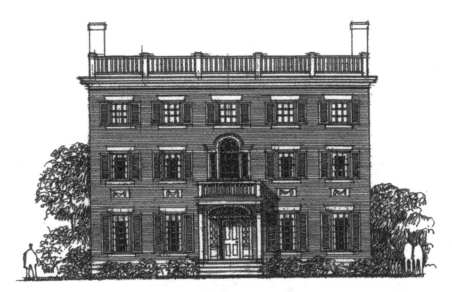

FEDERAL 1780–1820

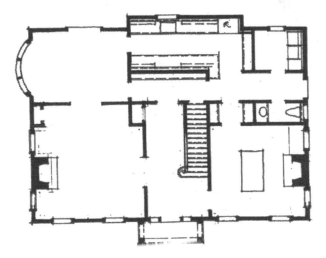

NEOCLASSICAL   1780–1825

Thomas Jefferson's architectural influence was pervasive throughout the former southern colonies, particularly in Virginia. Palladian
principles and proportions influenced Jefferson. His first version
of Monticello featured a double portico—Roman Doric below and
Ionic above—and was decidedly Palladian in spirit.

*Thomas Jefferson's first
version of Monticello,
1771*

Federal orders were usually attenuated—the columns elongated and
the entablatures often one-fifth the height of the column, instead of
the one-quarter as in Palladio's standards shown on pages 40–41.
The Neoclassicists, on the other hand, adhered strictly to the for-
mulae of "correct" proportion of the Roman prototypes and took few
liberties with established precedent.

Palladio, however, was no longer the single dominant source for
classical orders. Even Vitruvius was found to have edited and codified the Roman orders to suit himself. Archaeological discoveries
continued to reveal wider variety in classical orders than had been
previously supposed and the Neoclassicists drew from a wider selec-
tion of precedent. They rarely presumed to distort the proportions of
the classical orders except in the subtlest way. Angled bays and tall
windows, similar to the Federal buildings of the North, and articulated, symmetrical floor plans characterized the style. Introduced as a
Roman Revival but superseded by the late 1820s by the ubiquitous
Greek Revival, the style enjoyed a popular resurgence following the
Columbian Exposition in Chicago in 1893 (see page 104).

One encounters occasional vernacular examples of the Neoclassical style, invariably with badly proportioned forms. Any naive
attempt to imitate classical orders is the equivalent of pretentious
writing with no sense of grammar, syntax, or spelling.

NEOCLASSICAL 1780–1825

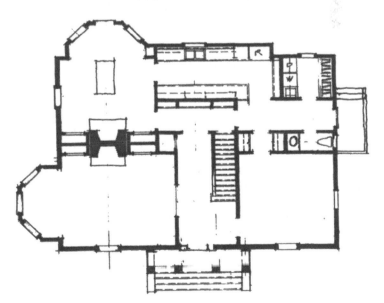

These two revival styles—the Greek and the Gothic—represent the double portal through which American architecture passed into a new age.

—Mary Mix Foley, *The American House*, 1979

5. AN EMERGING NATION   1820–1860

A British secret agent named Paul Wentworth reported at the end of the Revolution that "the American states comprise not one but three republics" and asserted that "the differences among these American republics were greater than between European states."* He referred to New England, the South, and the Middle Atlantic states.

Disparate as the new nation might be, a tremendous feeling of optimism prevailed in the generation born after the Declaration of Independence. The War of 1812 ended in 1815 with General Andrew Jackson's victory at the Battle of New Orleans. Britain's Napoleonic Wars came to an end as well and the seas were open once again to American shipping. Ports around the world were receptive to our fleets of clippers and America got on with the business of building a nation.

The vast Spanish empire was disintegrating. By 1819 the United States had acquired western Florida and the rest soon followed. Spain also surrendered its claim to the Pacific Northwest. By 1821 Mexico had won its independence and the Spanish lost all claim to North America. It was just a matter of time before the United States would control all the former Spanish territories north of the Rio Grande.

In 1823 the Monroe Doctrine gave expression to our sense of separateness from Europe—not just as a nation, but as a hemisphere. The American continents were "henceforth not to be considered as subjects for future colonization by any European powers." America was off limits; in return we would stay out of "internal concerns" of European nations. We felt no compunctions, however, about annexing Cuba and Texas a few years later. We developed a sense of chauvinistic pride and our manifest destiny was assured.

The predominant ethnic group in America at this time was still British in origin, though hardly cohesive. Initially immigration from Europe was light. Only 300,000 settlers came in the first forty years of independence. Less than five percent of the population in the first three decades of the nineteenth century resulted from immigration. After 1840, however, mass immigration increased, reaching a peak of three million people between 1845 and 1855. This was the

---

*Fisher, David Hackett. *Albion's Seed* (New York: Oxford University Press, 1989), p. 829.

greatest proportional influx ever and had an incalculable effect on
our society. Eighty-five percent of all immigrants between 1820 and
1860 came from Ireland, Germany, and Britain—in that order. (It is
interesting that in the last decade of this century less than twenty
percent of all Americans have any British ancestry. Today, more
Americans descend from German forebears than any other ethnic
group—slightly over twenty percent.)*

Most immigrants headed to urban areas. The Irish and many
Germans were Catholic. "Popery" was considered incompatible with
American freedom and Catholics were regarded with suspicion by
the established Protestant families. Many of the newcomers were
poor and were not easily assimilated. The components of our melting
pot began to arrive but, as H. L. Mencken caustically remarked in
the 1920s, "the only thing that melted was the pot."

For all the increase in our urban population, we were still an
agrarian society. Ninety-five percent lived on farms and towns remained small. "As late as 1860 only one city in the south had a
population of over 100,000; in 1840 only four cities west of the
coastal states had more than 10,000 people."†

We were also a restless nation. The movement west increased by
more than a third every ten years. The Erie Canal was completed in
1825 and the hinterland of America was suddenly more accessible
from the east. The first steamboat operated on the Mississippi in
1812. Cotton was never a viable export before that date and remained essentially a coastal crop until well after the War of 1812.
England imported 20,000,000 pounds of cotton in 1784—none of it
from the United States. That figure increased to 1.5 billion pounds in
1850 and 82 percent now came from the American South. In the
next decade that figure increased by two and half times and ac-
counted for more than all of our other exports combined.

Cotton quickly exhausted the soil and it was cheaper to buy new
land than to rotate crops. As Thomas Jefferson said, "It is cheaper for
Americans to buy new land than to manure the old." That land, of
course, lay in the "New South"—Alabama, Mississippi, and Louisiana.

With the diversity, growth, and energy of the early nineteenth
century, an interesting thing happened: we began to see ourselves as
the successors to the democracy of ancient Greece. Our Greek

*Ibid.
†Kennedy, Roger G., *Architecture, Men, Women, and Money* (Cambridge, MA:
MIT Press, 1989).

Revival style was surely the first national fad to sweep this country. Like most architectural movements here, it started in England following their archaeological discoveries of the mid-eighteenth century. Though these excavations kindled an interest in Greek architectural styles in Britain, the English never seriously adopted them to the extent that we did here. America felt both a kinship with the democratic ideals of the fifth century b.c. and an empathy with the modern Greeks who fought their own war of independence from the Turks between 1821 and 1830. Our taste for Greek architecture became almost a mania and the style was used for every building type from state capitols to privies. New towns that sprang up in western New York State and across the Appalachians boasted Greek names—Athens, Syracuse, Corinth, Sparta, and Ithaca, to name a few.

The Greek Revival was actually the culmination of the Neoclassicism which reached back before Rome to the original progenitor of the classical idiom: the Doric, the Ionic, and the Corinthian orders of the ancient Greeks. But the Greek Revival was essentially a rosy-hued and rather romanticized view of the Athenian world. One of the problems of embracing early Greece was the fact that it was a slave state and abolition of slavery was fast becoming a concern in the North. The importation of slaves had been abolished here in 1808 and England outlawed slavery in its colonies in 1833. The Greek Revival, however, became a national style between 1830 and 1850, and until 1860 in Alabama, Mississippi, and Louisiana when the Civil War interrupted building development.

Andrew Jackson was the first U.S. president to have come from "the people." He was the hero of the Battle of New Orleans in 1815 and was a popular president with whom the common people could identify. He was also the first president to have come of Scottish-Irish stock from the American backcountry frontier. The fact that General Jackson had actually lived in a log cabin was an appealing notion to most Americans; it was a theme that would be repeated by politicians in subsequent generations. His Tennessee house, The Hermitage, was a columned plantation house that fulfilled the idealized image of a proper Greek house (see page 53).

Benjamin Henry Latrobe (1764–1820) was one of our first architects. Born in England and trained on the continent, he emigrated to America in 1796. Though he has been credited with introducing the Greek Revival style to the United States with his Bank of Philadel-

Andalusia, Nicholas Biddle House near Philadelphia, Pennsylvania. Greek Revival additions to Benjamin Latrobe's 1806–7 design by Thomas U. Walter, 1833–41. This house in the Doric Order is one of the most noted Greek Revival houses in America.

Lyndhurst, Tarrytown, New York, by Alexander J. Davis, 1838–42, 1865–67. This is by far the largest of the Hudson River Gothic Revival houses.

phia in 1798, houses in the Greek mode did not appear much before the 1820s. John Haviland's *The Builder's Assistant* (1818, revised 1821) was the first American publication to detail the ancient Greek orders. Asher Benjamin revised his *The American Builder's Companion* in 1827 and Minard Lafever published *The Modern Builder's Guide* and *The Beauties of Modern Architecture* in the 1830s. These books stressed the merits of the Greek style. They were widely disseminated and were largely responsible for the consistency of design whenever the classical Greek mode appeared.

The architectural profession grew increasingly important during this period. There was a growing need for public buildings as more states were added to the Union and the population increased. William Strickland (1788–1854), Ithiel Town (1784–1844), and Alexander Jackson Davis (1803–1899) (who practiced with Town) all used Greek forms. Davis later became enamored of the Picturesque styles; his Gothic Revival work appeared in his *Rural Residences* in 1837 and in Andrew Jackson Downing's *Victorian Cottage Residences* and *The Architecture of Country Houses,* both published in the 1840s.

One of the problems with classical architecture in general, and the Greek Revival in particular, was its lack of flexible forms. Essentially the style depended on the basic temple form and it could not effectively serve all the demands that American building placed upon it. It was a prescribed way of building with the same concern with precedent that had affected the Georgian architects a few generations before. The flexibility and "fitness of purpose" of the Gothic Revival and the Italianate styles were much more suitable to varied building complexes and creative massing of disparate forms. Sentiment also began to shift in the 1840s from the romance of ancient Greece to the romance of the Middle Ages.

The Gothic style was seen a generation earlier in England, around 1800, as a Christian style—suitable for a Christian (Anglican) nation. It had a moral tone. Somehow, if one lived in a Gothic style— that is, a Christian style—house, it would be conducive to leading a moral life. That notion was prevalent here as well and in the 1840s the Gothic Revival challenged the Greek Revival.

GREEK REVIVAL 1820–1850

Greek architecture was based on post and beam construction and never featured the arch or dome so prominent in Roman building. Greek temple architecture evolved in the fifth century B.C. with the development of the Doric, Ionic, and Corinthian orders. Though the latter was similar to the Roman, the Doric and Ionic were somewhat more ponderous than their later versions. The Greek Doric was only 7½ lower diameters in height and had no base block at the foot of the column. (Compare this with the Roman Doric shown on page 40.)

Greek Revival houses usually oriented the gable end toward the road. The roof pitch was lower than that in colonial houses and was too shallow to permit dormers. The eave line was usually raised a couple of feet above the attic floor and hopper windows were designed to fit in the frieze just below the cornice. Light and ventilation were provided in the attic by these low windows. Recessed entrances with wide casings were common and usually featured sidelights and rectangular transoms. Houses were usually either columned or embellished with pilasters.

Though Greek temples were actually polychrome, Greek Revival houses were always painted white. The symbolic purity of the stark white house had universal appeal. The white clapboard house with dark-green louvered blinds became a popular craze during the Greek Revival period and has persisted to this day in the mistaken notion that such a house is "colonial." The southern plantation house, idealized in the movie version of *Gone with the Wind* (though not in the book) was a columned temple form—an example of the Greek Revival style.

Tara, from the movie
Gone with the Wind

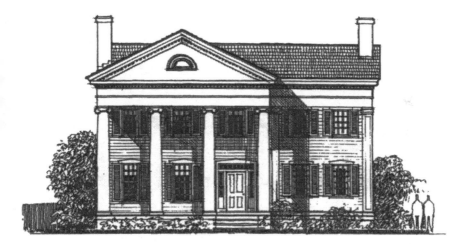

GREEK REVIVAL 1820–1850

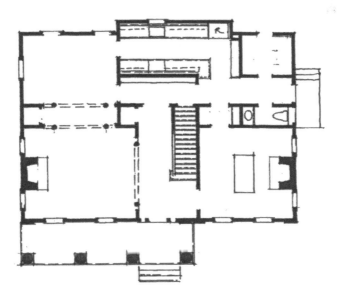

GOTHIC REVIVAL   1840–1860

Sir Horace Walpole converted his country house Strawberry Hill in Twickenham, near London, to a somewhat fanciful and superficial version of a "Gothick" building in 1750. It heralded a taste for the romance of the Middle Ages instead of the ancient world. Sir Walter Scott's novels and his own hodgepodge of medieval fiction, Abbotsford (in Scotland not far from the English border), were widely admired on both sides of the Atlantic.

Strawberry Hill, Twickenham, England, 1750–1776

Andrew Jackson Downing, the great taste maker of the 1840s, promoted the Gothic Revival in his books on "cottage villas" published in the 1840s. The Hudson River Valley was the perfect setting for the kind of picturesque, rambling, "irregular" designs he endorsed. Here the ecclesiastical associations were less important than they were in Britain, and the Gothic was seen by anglophiles here as simply an English style. It was the first of the so-called Picturesque styles and symbolized a time of chivalry, of a romance with the past in a world that was becoming increasingly mercantile and a time that wasn't always so nice.

The Gothic Revival is appealing not as much for its stylistic embellishments as for its more organic approach to design. The late Gothic builders of the Tudor period were less concerned with formal, stylistic dogma than they were with the celebration of craft and utility. The Gothic Revival leads much more directly to a kind of rational shaping of space that is an expression of the interior spaces.

Steeply pitched roofs with cross gables featuring carved verge boards (sometimes called barge-boards) along the rakes and hood moldings over the tall, diamond-paned windows identify the style. Vertical siding with earthy tones was common and verandahs and balconies embellished with brackets and railings featuring an exuberance of Gothic detail.

GOTHIC REVIVAL 1840–1860

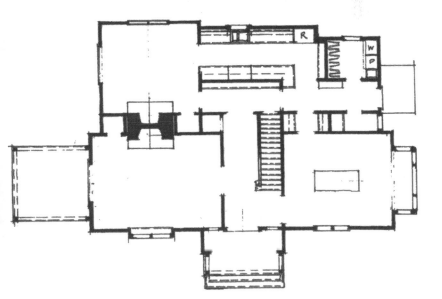

The mingled quaintness, beauty, and picturesqueness of the exterior . . . when harmoniously complete, seem to transport one back to a past age, the domestic habits, the hearty hospitality, the joyous old sports, and the romance and chivalry of which, invest it, in the dim retrospect, with a kind of golden glow, in which the shadowy lines of poetry and reality seem strangely interwoven and blended.

—A. J. Downing, *Victorian Cottage Residences,* 1842

6. THE PICTURESQUE   1840–1900

The Picturesque movement was an expression of a nineteenth-century philosophy of architecture and landscape design. It derived from landscape paintings by artists who emphasized the harmony and integration of man, buildings, and nature. Nicolas Poussin and Claude Lorrain were mid-seventeenth-century painters whose works were particularly admired for their picturesque qualities and were a source of picturesque theory. Many of the styles that evolved from this movement have been associated with the Victorian era.

The Gothic was the harbinger of the Picturesque styles. Real Gothic architecture of the twelfth, thirteenth, and fourteenth centuries derived its intrinsic style from an expression of its structural system. Walpole's "Gothick" Strawberry Hill was a new costume for a fancy dress ball. The detailing had little or nothing to do with the actual structure. His house was widely publicized and initiated a fascination with the Gothic style that found its way to our shores in the 1840s. The Greek Revival and the Gothic Revival were the styles that bridged the change from the end of the Renaissance age to the new industrial era of the modern world.

Cronkhill, a small agent's house at Attingham Park in Shropshire designed by John Nash (1752–1835) in 1802, was a key example of the Picturesque in the form of a rural Italian villa. It was the first interpretation of an idealized vernacular farmhouse from the popular picturesque landscapes and became the prototype of Italianate villas in America.

The classicism of the eighteenth century—whether rigidly orthodox or loosely interpreted and adapted to residential scale—was no longer the only accepted architectural mode. Words like "irregular," "adaptability," "informal," and "fitness of purpose" became the slogans of the new Picturesque movement. The idea of a house in the country became increasingly important for the English middle class. The retreat, the romantic hideaway, and the pastoral shooting lodge all satisfied a need of the successful mercantile class on both sides of the Atlantic to escape from the realities of the source of their money. This rejection of the formal, imposing, classical house opened up all kinds of possibilities for inspiration and emulation.

The English publication of E. Gyfford's *Designs for Elegant Cottages and Small Villas and Small Picturesque Cottages and Hunting Boxes* in 1806 and J. B. Popworth's *Rural Residences* in 1818 reflected an increasing predilection for the quaint among the English middle class. These books nurtured a taste for the Gothic retreat, the Swiss chalet, the Italian farmhouse, and the "cottage orné." With such variety of style, unity was achieved in a cohesiveness of scale, planning, and respect for the garden park.

Nineteenth-century England paid a tremendous price in social ills for its industrial and commercial growth. The order, grace, and dignity of the earlier Georgian era succumbed to a world of squalor, human exploitation, and industrial blight. There were social reformers—Charles Dickens, for one—who reacted against this new reality. The English Arts and Crafts movement, encouraged by William Morris (1834–1896), flourished in Victoria's reign after 1860 and in this country after 1890. It was also a response to the negative aspects of the times and took the form of a romantic revival of the arts and crafts of an idealized past. People sought Ye Olde England, the good old days in an attempt to ignore the unpleasant realities of the present.

One positive force was a movement in domestic architecture toward a house for the then-modern age. In 1859 the designer William Morris commissioned Phillip Webb (1831–1915) to design a house near London. The result, The Red House, was seen by Hermann Muthesius as "the first private house of the new artistic culture, the first house to be conceived and built as a unified whole inside and out, the very first example in the history of the modern house."*

The Red House,
William Morris's house in Bexley Heath, Kent, by Philip Webb, 1859

*Muthesius, Hermann, *The English House* (Berlin: 1904; New York: Rizzoli International Publications, 1979).

The Red House set the tone for the work of Norman Shaw, W. E. Nesfield, E. W. Godwin, B. Champneys, and J. J. Stevenson. They were prominent among the principal architects in the so-called Queen Anne movement in the latter half of the nineteenth century. The term Queen Anne is really a misnomer and should not be confused with the Renaissance style that prevailed during the first fifteen years of the eighteenth century. The Victorian term, as Mark Girouard put it in his excellent book *Sweetness and Light—The Queen Anne Movement 1860–1900*, "was a kind of architectural cocktail, with a little genuine Queen Anne in it, a little Flemish, a squeeze of Robert Adam, a generous dash of Wren, and a touch of François I."* Though mostly for rich clients, this new architecture was less pompous than the classical and, with the use of warm red brick, sash windows, and a Dutch intimacy of scale, provided the source for much of the American Picturesque architecture toward the end of the nineteenth century. It is important to note that the American Queen Anne style quickly developed a very different character·from the English. To call it the American Queen Anne would be a bit laborious but more appropriate.

Manor Farm, Hampstead, by Basil Champneys, 1881, is an example of English Queen Anne.

William Carson House, Eureka, California, by Samuel and Joseph Newsome, begun 1884, is the quintessential American Queen Anne.

*Girouard, Mark, *The Queen Anne Movement 1860–1900* (Oxford: The Clarendon Press, 1977; New Haven, CT: Yale University Press, 1984).

*Sezincote, Colonel John Cockerell's house in Gloustershire
by his brother S. P. Cockerell, c. 1803*

Royal Pavilion at Brighton by John Nash, c. 1818

Queen Victoria succeeded George IV in 1837 and ruled until January 1900. Her name has been associated with architecture throughout that entire era even more in this country than it is in Britain. The diversity of styles and character makes the term "Victorian style" almost meaningless. There are no less than eight distinct styles that are called Victorian in popular parlance, and many vernacular combinations could also be added to the list. In addition to the Gothic Revival, the list includes the Swiss Cottage, the Italianate styles, Exotic Eclectic, Second Empire, the Stick style, and the Queen Anne. One of the aims of this chapter is to sort out the principal styles that come under the general term Victorian so that each one can be appreciated for its own particular qualities.

William Watts Sherman House, Newport, Rhode Island, by Henry Hobson Richardson, 1874, often considered the first American Queen Anne

Griswold House, Newport, Rhode Island, by Richard Morris Hunt, 1863

SWISS COTTAGE   1840–1860

There is probably no more "picturesque" country anywhere, even today, than Switzerland. In his 1823 book *Rural Architecture, or a Series of Designs for Ornamental Cottages,* the Englishman P. F. Robinson recommended the Swiss Cottage style for residential designs. Andrew Jackson Downing suggested the Swiss Cottage style in his *Victorian Cottage Residences,* saying that anyone "fond of the wild and picturesque, whose home chances to be in some one of our rich mountain valleys, may give it a peculiar interest by imitating the Swiss Cottage, or at least its expressive and striking features."

For the English Switzerland was "Protestant and clean." It represented an idyllic land remote from their growing industrialization. Dickens had a small chalet in his garden and Queen Victoria imported one in 1853 as a playhouse at Osbourne, her retreat on the Isle of Wight. There is even a tube stop on the London Underground that commemorates an 1840 tavern built in the style near St. John's Wood. Few Swiss cottages survive from the nineteenth century. The decorative details of the style, however, inspired much of the "gingerbread" which encrusted vernacular interpretations of the various Victorian styles.

In our era there is a perfect parallel to this escapist mentality. Vermont's Stratton Mountain was developed as a ski area in the early 1960s and nurtured an Austrian theme. The ski school was Austrian and Tyrolean music contributed to the atmosphere. Most of the "chalets" (not "ski lodges") looked like cuckoo clocks. They had shallow pitched roofs and typically a second-floor balcony beneath a gabled overhang. The railings had flat board balustrades with cutout decorative motifs. Heraldic shields abounded. This storybook architecture provides an escape from the world of business for the city executive today much as it did for his counterpart in the Victorian age.

*Swiss Cottage
from Andrew Jackson Downing's*
The Architecture of
Country Houses *(1850)*

SWISS COTTAGE 1840–1860

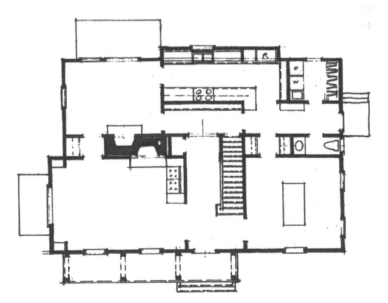

ITALIAN VILLA   1845-1870

John Nash designed Cronkhill in 1802. Other Italianate houses based on the vernacular styles of northern Italy soon followed. They became increasingly popular in England and of course soon caught on here. Andrew Jackson Downing was the great proponent of the style.

In *Victorian Cottage Residences,* published in 1842, Downing wrote, "an Italian villa may recall, to one familiar with Italy and art, by its bold roof lines, its campanile and its shady balconies, the classic beauty of that fair and smiling land." He also suggested that the "irregular" villa, through its "variety," would evoke in "persons who have cultivated an architectural taste . . . a great preference to a design capable of awakening more strongly emotions of the beautiful or picturesque, as well as the useful or convenient."

The villa as an English house type evolved in the eighteenth century but found great popularity in the Regency period of 1811-1820. Larger than a cottage and more cohesive than most farmhouses, the scale of a villa was appropriate for a family residence generally set on a modest amount of land near a city.

The tower is the key feature of this style and distinguishes it from the Italianate. Both styles have shallow pitched roofs with broad overhangs decorated with carved brackets. Wall textures are usually smooth, reflecting the original stuccoed surfaces. Tall windows, often with rounded tops with prominent crown moldings, and informal compositions with loggias and verandahs are typical of the style. The Italian Villa style was inspired by the buildings in the painted landscapes of the French Romanticists Lorrain and Poussin.

Cronkhill
Attingham Park, Shropshire,
by John Nash, 1802

ITALIAN VILLA 1845–1870

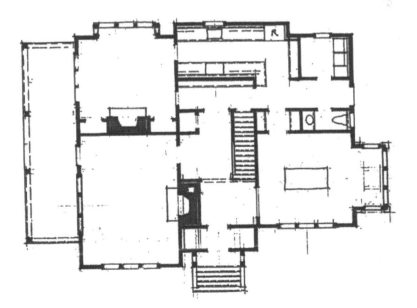

ITALIANATE   1845–1875

The Italianate style was akin to the Italian Villa but did not feature a tower. So popular was it during the 1850s and 1860s that it was even called the American Bracketed style. (It was also called the Tuscan, Lombard, and simply the American style.)

The decorative brackets that adorn the eaves of the Italianate house immediately identify the style. They were simple consoles either evenly spaced or often paired. The basic Italianate house style was less complex than the Italian Villa style, and brackets and verandahs were often added to older farmhouses to give them a stylish uplift. Many Italianate houses were almost square in plan with high ceilings. The shallow-pitched hip roofs were often capped with a cupola or lantern at the very top. The attic was apt to have a row of awning windows between the eave brackets, not only creating additional head room but also making for a cool house in summer when the breezes could blow through the cupola windows and draw cooler air through the low attic openings.

An eccentric named Orson Squire Fowler wrote a book called *The Octagon House: A Home for All* which was published in 1848 and revised in 1853. He was responsible for a modest fad which swept across the country for fifteen or twenty years. Some architectural writers designate the octagon house as a separate style. It is actually a building type, and most octagon houses were built in a simple version of the Italianate style. Fowler's book is most entertaining and is in fact full of sensible advice about building an efficient and practical house.

An octagon house, c. 1860

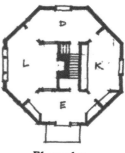

Floor plan

ITALIANATE 1845–1875

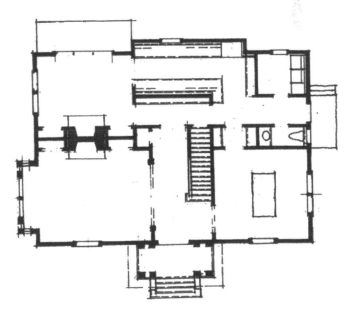

ITALIAN RENAISSANCE REVIVAL   1845–1860

It may seem odd to include this revival in a group of Picturesque styles. Not all houses have to be quaint, however, to be worthy of portraiture. Though less fanciful than other popular styles it is just as much a Victorian style and warrants inclusion.

Sir Charles Barry (1795–1860) designed the Traveller's Club built in London in 1819 and it became the prototype of this Victorian revival style. Simple flat facades, rectangular forms, and restrained decorative features characterize the style. Surface textures were smooth limestone or stucco. What columns were used were often limited to the entrance porch. The assertive cornice was proportioned to the overall height of the building. For example, if the Ionic order was used in the cornice, its height would be approximately one-thirteenth the height of the building from its base to the top of the cornice. Balustrade balconies, string courses, and tall windows extending almost to the floor on the main level were common features. The style was used for men's clubs throughout the second half of the nineteenth century, and every town with any British roots that boasted an athenaeum would have built it in this style. Infrequently used for freestanding houses, it was and remained an urban or at least a town style.

Perhaps the best examples of the Italian Renaissance Revival are the brownstones built as blocks of row houses in New York City as Manhattan expanded northward after the Civil War. Three landmark examples of the style are the Philadelphia Athenaeum (1847), India House in New York City (1850), and the post office in Georgetown, Washington, D.C., which was built as the customs house in 1857. Though none is residential, each has the scale and character of a substantial house. This is perhaps the only style of the period that exuded refinement with minimal use of columns for decoration.

Post Office
(former Custom House)
Gerogetown, Washington, D.C.

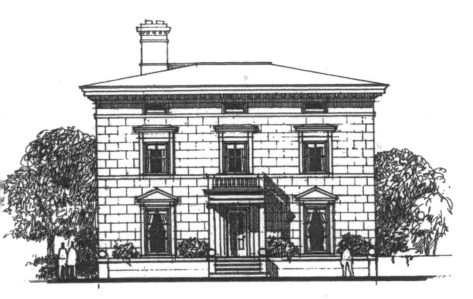

ITALIAN RENAISSANCE REVIVAL 1845–1860

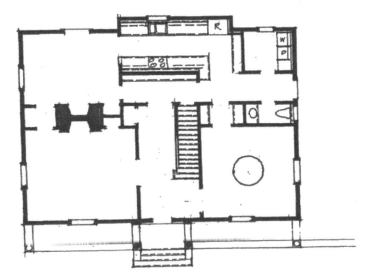

EXOTIC ECLECTIC   1850–1875

Most Picturesque houses in the nineteenth century drew from precedents in the dim and distant past. The love of the Picturesque was so widespread and fashionable that no one considered the construction of a folly or fake ruin as eccentric. Rather, one had to create something especially bizarre to appear exotic.

This romance with the past soon expanded to include stylistic elements of remote lands. Moorish bazaars, Indian palaces, Turkish mosques, and Oriental harems — alone or in combination — inspired many fanciful houses. The British have always respected eccentricity — particularly among the upper classes; Americans have generally viewed it with suspicion. But we have had our share of eccentric houses.

In 1803 S. P. Cockerell designed Sezincote in Gloucestershire for a retired nabob of the East India Company. It was complete with onion domes, minarets, and a flavor of India. John Nash's design for the Prince Regent's Brighton Pavilion built between 1815 and 1822 was the apotheosis of Picturesque fantasy. It was an Indian dream palace featuring a colossal assemblage of Islamic domes. (See page 72.)

My favorite American contributions to Exotic Eclecticism are Samuel Sloan's Longwood and Frederick Church's Olana with its Moorish embellishments. The first was an unfinished 1862 octagon near Nanchez, Mississippi, and the other an 1874 fantasy overlooking the Hudson River in New York.

Longwood, 1862   *Olana, 1874*

EXOTIC ECLECTIC 1850–1875

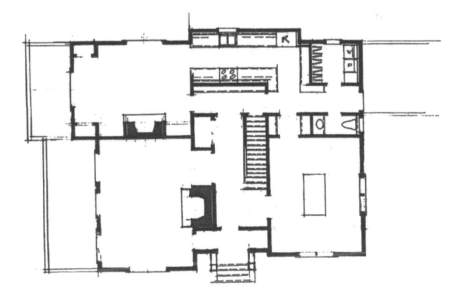

SECOND EMPIRE   1860–1880

Napoleon III (Louis Napoleon Bonaparte), Napoleon I's nephew, became president of France in 1848. He appeared to practically all the French people as a chauvinistic leader on a white horse who would champion their interests over corrupt political opportunists. Limited by the French constitution to one term, in 1851 he summarily dismissed the assembly and seized power in a coup d'etat. After declaring himself emperor, he remained head of state for almost ten years.

Louis Napoleon transformed the old Paris into the city of grand boulevards that we know today. He enlarged the Louvre between 1852 and 1857 and set the fashion for a new style. The mansard roof is the single key feature of the Second Empire style. It is a double-pitched hip roof with large dormer windows on the steep lower slope. The eave is commonly defined by substantial moldings and supported by Italianate brackets. There are also moldings capping both the top of the first roof slope and the upper slope; the upper part of the roof usually intersects with a flat roof over the middle of the building. The effect of this construction was an entire usable floor at the attic level. Named for the seventeenth-century architect François Mansart (1598–1666), the mansard roof's enlarged attic supposedly provided an additional rental floor in Parisian tenements where the zoning ordinance limited the number of stories.

It is puzzling that the official architectural style of an authoritarian government would appeal to Americans. However, a mansard roof now seems perfectly natural on a Vermont farmhouse. The style remained extremely popular for twenty years before it was superseded by the Colonial Revival styles after 1876.

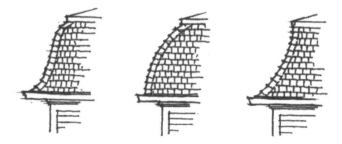

Typical mansard roof profiles

SECOND EMPIRE 1860–1880

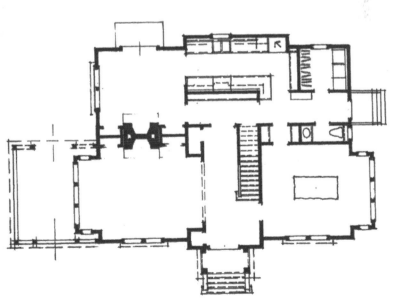

STICK   1855–1875

The Gothic Revival, the Swiss Cottage, and the Italianate styles found impetus in European precedent. They were the initial Picturesque styles. American designers soon created a new style, however, that sought character from complexity of form and an inventive expression of structure. In his *Village and Farm Cottages* published in 1856, Henry W. Cleaveland captured the essence of this new and energetic way of building: "The strength and character of the new style depends almost wholly on the shadows which are thrown upon its surface by projecting members." Cleaveland did not use the term Stick style; that term was coined by Yale professor Vincent J. Scully, Jr., a hundred years later.

The character of this style derives basically from steeply pitched roofs and vaguely Elizabethan vestiges. The celebration of structure in the flamboyant projections, brackets, and rafter tails was reinforced by the playfully sculptural quality. Sometimes evident are fancy decorative details that were either invented wholly or derived from such diverse sources as Swiss cottages and Oriental temples.

The principal feature of the Stick style is the pattern of wood boards—vertical, horizontal, and sometimes diagonal—that suggests a structural framework beneath the clapboard skin. This Elizabethan half-timbered appearance may, in fact, not articulate the actual structure, for balloon frame construction was in common use by the 1850s and the suggestion of a braced frame is somewhat illusory. It was a very popular style for churches during this twenty-year period; indeed most towns on eastern Long Island have one.

Gervase Wheeler's *Rural Homes* was published in eight editions between 1851 and 1869. It did much to promote the Stick style. Even Richard Morris Hunt, best known for his French Chateaux, designed perhaps the most famous Stick style house of all: the Griswold House in Newport, Rhode Island, built in 1863.

Griswold House,
Newport, Rhode Island,
by Richard Morris Hunt, 1863

STICK 1855–1875

QUEEN ANNE   1880–1910

The Queen Anne style is almost the quintessential style of Norman Rockwell's America. Popular in its heyday, it has recently been rediscovered and is often celebrated with wild "boutique" colors. The style evolved in England as an outgrowth of the Arts and Crafts movement of the mid-nineteenth century. The British government built two half-timbered buildings at the Philadelphia Centennial Exposition in 1876. These structures were the impetus for the Queen Anne style in this country.

Henry Hobson Richardson's William Watts Sherman house built in Newport, Rhode Island, in 1874 is usually considered the first Queen Anne house by an American architect. It featured quasi-medieval half-timbering, assertive chimneys, and a varied but cohesive surface pattern—all deftly handled by one of our great architects. The style quickly became popular here but was not favored by architects. They generally preferred the Shingle style which evolved from some of the same sources but used a more cogent vocabulary. The Queen Anne style was promoted in publications like the *American Architect and Building News,* our first architectural magazine, and was sold precut by mail-order companies. Components like knee braces, brackets, and spindles were also shipped across the country to embellish older vernacular houses.

The American Queen Anne differed from the English in its exuberant use of scroll work and applied detail. The English built brick houses and Americans wood. The Carson House in California, begun in 1884, is the ultimate example of the style (see page 71). Floor plans were usually open and free-flowing. Double parlor doors were popular as were corner fireplaces. America's love affair with the porch or verandah found fulfillment in the Queen Anne style. Turrets, towers, and fanciful gazebos characterized the style along with varied shingle patterns and wall surfaces. One cannot call it *the* Victorian style—it is simply one of many.

The term Eastlake is sometimes confused with Queen Anne. In the 1870s and 1880s decorative components were mass produced by mechanical lathes and jigsaws and were used to embellish eclectic houses with fancy scrollwork, turned ballusters and porch posts, beaded spindles, and sometimes even wrought-iron embellishments. The English interior designer Charles Locke Eastlake (1833–1906) disassociated himself from the style that bears his name.

QUEEN ANNE 1880–1910

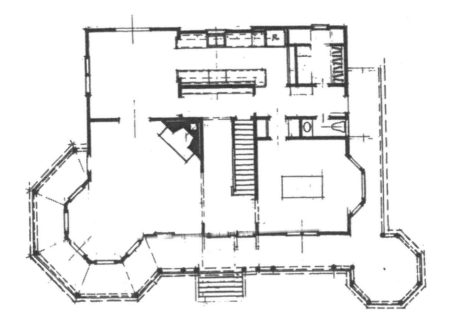

Not the Truth, but a big bankroll will make you free. And being free you can build whatever you want.

—Alan Gowans, *The Comfortable House,* 1986

7. PALATIAL PALACES   1880–1930

In 1870 America had a population of forty million and over seventy five percent still lived in rural areas. The full impact of the industrial revolution was still to be felt, and the next forty years would be a period of enormous change. By 1910 the population had more than doubled and almost half lived in cities and large towns. The economic diversity of the country had never been greater nor the complexities of our social structure more intricate.

"Between 1870 and 1900, the national wealth quadrupled (rising from $30,400 million to $126,700 million and doubled again by 1914—reaching $254,200)." In 1892 "the Census Bureau estimated that 9 per cent of the nation's families owned 71 per cent of the wealth."*

With the influx of immigrants from abroad as well as the movement to the cities from rural areas, our urban areas underwent traumatic change. Ghettos formed in the inner cities, the suburbs burgeoned for the middle and upper classes, and resorts and enclaves were created for those who could afford the price. All this emphasized the strata of our society—our differences rather than our similarities. Technology and industry supported these changes. The railroad had perhaps the greatest effect for it was both a physical network of steel that bound the country together and a reflection of a restless mobility unprecedented in the history of mankind. Local commuter railroads like Philadelphia's "Main Line" transformed rural farmland into areas of impressive estates that were synonymous with privilege and upper-class status. The automobile wasn't far behind in reinforcing this rural mobility and solving what might have been one of the drawbacks of living apart from one's neighbors.

Electricity, central heating, indoor plumbing, the telephone, the typewriter, and the washing machine all became commonplace in this era—and not just for the very rich. The American suburban "four-square" and the bungalow soon sprouted up throughout the new suburbs and small towns. Sears, Roebuck and Company, Aladdin Redi-Cut Houses, and other companies sold thousands of modest precut houses and shipped them by rail all over the country. In his excellent book *The Comfortable House*, Alan Gowans pointed out

*Baltzell, E. Digby, *The Protestant Establishment* (New York: Vintage, 1966).

that between 1890 and 1930, "thanks to partial or total prefabrica-
tion, more houses were erected than in the nation's entire previous
history."* Most of these modest houses incorporated the same
amenities mentioned above and indeed provided a level of comfort
never really known before, regardless of the income level of the
owner.

Typical Four-Square

Even with the great diversity of architectural styles there was a
search for order, unity, and structure—reassurance that this incredibly disparate land had a worthy history, a legitimate social order, and
a class hierarchy that reflected that order. Above the fray of na-
tionalistic pride stimulated by our centennial celebration in 1876
stood a newly formed social class bound together by enormous
wealth. Many within this group sought comfort and reassurance
from the power of their new-found money. Entrée into exclusive
clubs, societies, and boards of philanthropic organizations—
hospitals, schools, universities, and religious foundations—was a
conspicuous reward for the work ethic and an almost Calvinistic
confirmation that one was a member of God's elect.

It was in the form of their houses that many of these "elect" chose
to display the evidence of their material success. In this same era the
Shingle style and the Colonial Revival were emerging, but these
styles were not ostentatious enough for the more blatant show-offs
and were only built by people who were less inclined to display their
material success so conspicuously.

Richard Morris Hunt; McKim, Mead & White; and Warren &
Wetmore were architectural firms that served immensely wealthy
clients. The apotheosis of the palatial palace was G. W. Vanderbilt's
chateau Biltmore, designed by Hunt and built in Ashville, North

*Gowans, Alan, *The Comfortable House* (Cambridge, MA: MIT Press, 1986).

Carolina, in 1893. It cost over half of his inheritance which was rumored to have been $6,000,000. Hunt had designed several Chateauesque houses for other members of the Vanderbilt family. Mark Twain's "Gilded Age" was in full bloom. This was the era of the "Four Hundred," and there was a pervasive determination among the new social class to establish an aristocracy of wealth. Daughters were married off to titled Europeans and the Social Register was first published in 1887 to be sure that everyone knew who everyone was and what they belonged to. But most revealing was the architectural expression of the age, in which was an implicit desire for social stability. Besides the Chateauesque, the most popular opulent styles were the Romanesque, Beaux-Arts, Tudor, Second Italian Renaissance Revival, and Neoclassical Revival. There were ample Colonial Revival and even Shingle style houses of considerable size (the Goelet house in Newport, Rhode Island, for example), but they tended to be more restrained and were not used if one wanted to really show off. Let's see why each of these styles was so well suited to its purpose.

The Robert Goelet House,
Newport, Rhode Island, by McKim, Mead & White, 1882

ROMANESQUE   1880–1900

Perhaps "Richardsonian Romanesque" would be a better term for this style. Henry Hobson Richardson (1838–1886) graduated from Harvard in 1859 and then became the second American to study at the Ecole des Beaux-Arts in Paris. He began his practice in New York in 1865. In 1872 he won the competition for Trinity Church in Boston and moved his practice there. The rectory of the church was the first house ever built here in the Romanesque style.

Not a style for the masses, this pre-Gothic or English Norman style mandated masonry construction. The massive rusticated walls and semicircular arches made these houses expensive to build. Never a popular residential style, even for those who could afford it, Romanesque houses were built for wealthy industrialists who considered the fanciful chateaux and the Beaux-Arts classicism too arty or frivolous for their tastes. Several Romanesque houses were built in St. Louis, Chicago, Philadelphia, and New York in the 1880s and 1890s. A retrospective monograph of Richardson's work was published in 1888 and gave impetus to the style, but the Columbian Exposition in Chicago in 1893 was an effective advertisement for Beaux-Arts classicism.

The most obvious characteristics of the Romanesque style are the massive ashlar stonework, the half-round arches with neatly cut voussoirs, and the bold and simple massing. Windows are mostly 1 over 1 with masonry mullions and transom bars. Even with its turrets and multigabled composition, the style is more of a massive masonry version of the contemporaneous Shingle style than the more extravagant Queen Anne.

Though the Romanesque style was rarely used for freestanding houses, one can find occasional row houses with Romanesque facades built of brownstone or Roman brick with terra-cotta details.

Ames Gate Lodge,
North Easton, Massachusetts,
by Henry Hobson Richardson,
1882–83

ROMANESQUE 1880–1900

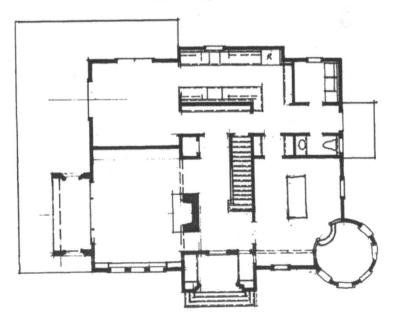

CHATEAUESQUE   1885–1910

Francis I became king of France in 1515, just six years after Henry VIII ascended the throne of England. They both died in 1547. Most of the famous chateaux that were the models for our Chateauesque style were built during Francis I's reign. Chambord, Blois, and Chenonçeaux are perhaps the best known; they all combined the late Gothic style of fifteenth-century France with the new Italian Renaissance details just being introduced in France.

Although Richard Morris Hunt returned to the United States from Paris before our Civil War, not even the most extravagant of his clients were ready for so opulent and palatial a style until the 1880s. At that time, however, it became the ultimate style for the conspicuous display of wealth.

Too extravagant to be mannered in wood, Chateauesque mansions were built of either smooth, flat Roman brick with narrow mortar joints or smooth limestone. The dominant, steeply pitched roof was a stylistic reference to the French Gothic as were the hood molds above the windows and doors and the vestige of tracery featured in the pierced railings of the balconies. The characteristic "basket handle" arch above the front door was also a late Gothic detail and was a common feature of the Chateauesque style. In contrast, the horizontal string courses, pilasters, and the occasional round arch were all Renaissance in origin.

So-called wall dormers—upper-story extensions of the exterior wall that interrupt the continuity of the eave line—were characteristic of the style as interpreted in the late nineteenth and early twentieth centuries. Roof dormers were commonly used as well. Rounded turrets, decorated pinnacles, and assertively fanciful chimneys combined with spires, finials, and ornamental iron railings to identify the style. Besides Hunt's Biltmore, smaller examples can be found in St. Louis, Chicago, outside of Philadelphia, and in Newport, Rhode Island.

CHATEAUESQUE 1885–1910

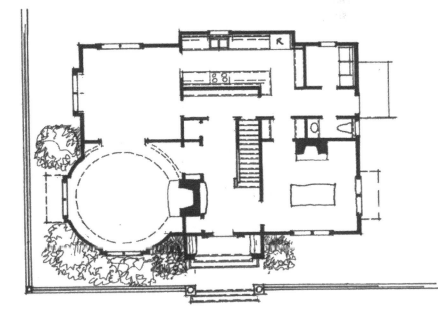

BEAUX-ARTS   1890–1930

The Ecole des Beaux-Arts in Paris was founded in the early eighteenth century and was the premier architectural school of the nineteenth century. America's first school of architecture was founded at MIT in 1865. It was soon followed by Cornell, Syracuse, Michigan, and Columbia. All were patterned on the Paris prototype. But a year or so in Paris was still considered an impressive social as well as academic credential for most American architects—even those who already held degrees.

By the late nineteenth century the school had a long-established approach to design. The curriculum instilled in the students a feeling for grandiose axial formality in both planning and composition, articulation of building mass, and a predilection for pictorial extravagance. The magnificently rendered presentations in plan, section, and elevation captured the essence of their educational goal.

Heavy stone basements, coupled columns, grand staircases, decorative swags, shields and garlands, and freestanding statuary all help to identify the style.

In an era of rapid change and great diversity, the ordered symmetry of the Beaux-Arts formality lent a sense of unity to an otherwise disparate society. The Columbian Exposition in Chicago in 1893 was a triumph of the Beaux-Arts classicism and was seen as the unveiling of an American Renaissance. Classical forms, extravagant, yet controlled by Hunt's cohesive plan, appealed to the successful businessmen of the day. Here the authority of French sophistication nurtured the Gilded Age. In 1879 Mark Twain had observed that the French "citizen requires 'glory'—that is the main thing; plenty of glory, plenty of noise, plenty of show, . . . plenty of masked balls and fantastic nonsense." But of course not everyone liked Twain.

BEAUX-ARTS 1890–1930

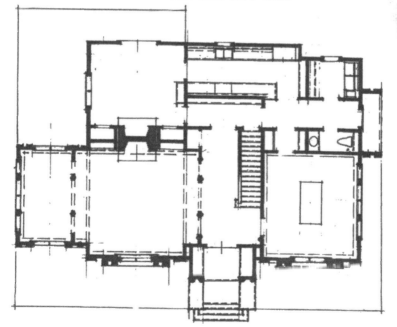

TUDOR   1890–1930

Some architectural writers call any house inspired by the English Tudor, Elizabethan, and Jacobean (for James I) period "Jacobethan" or even "Tudorbethan." I have always thought those terms a little patronizing. When used for buildings on college campuses in the 1920s this style was often called "Collegiate Gothic" which somehow seems less patronizing. One wonders why the style was not called Neo-Tudor or Tudor Revival.

Elizabeth I was the daughter of Henry Tudor—that is, Henry VIII. She died in 1603 and was the last of the Tudor line. Technically, then, Jacobean architecture was not Tudor even though the styles have much in common. This guide uses the term Tudor for masonry or stucco buildings, Elizabethan for half-timbered structures, and Jacobean for masonry structures with Dutch or Flemish gables. Though a bit of an oversimplification, this terminology is prevalent and helps to keep the styles straight.

The Tudor parapeted gables, large leaded windows detailed with stone mullions and transoms, and the characteristic Tudor arch all help to identify this style. Projecting oriel window bays were common in the originals and were incorporated into these early twentieth-century neo-Tudor houses.

Remember that at the turn of the century the predominant ethnic group in the United States was still British in origin. The successful businessman who chose to build a substantial house could easily identify with the early English manor house and all its associated values. The Beaux-Arts and Chateauesque styles were too affected for many solid Anglo-Saxon Protestants, and the Romanesque, though certainly masculine, failed to evoke the image of the English landed gentry that seemed the inevitable reward for a successful businessman with British roots. By the 1930s the Tudor style had become a symbol of success for persons of any ethnic background.

TUDOR 1890–1930

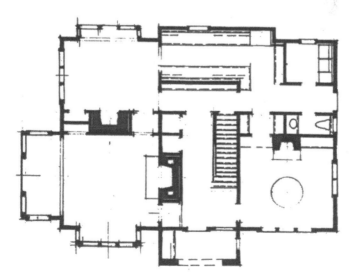

SECOND ITALIAN RENAISSANCE REVIVAL 1890–1930

This was the first of the so-called "Mediterranean" styles and was based on the palaces of the sixteenth- and seventeenth-century Italian Renaissance. Symmetrical stone or stuccoed structures with red tiled hip roofs and substantial cornices supported with brackets or consoles were typical of these houses. They generally had more varied facades than houses of the early Italian Renaissance Revival of the mid-nineteenth century. Entrances were often marked with either a projecting portico or a recessed loggia emphasized with an arched Palladian motif.

The Villard house (1887) in New York by McKim, Mead & White was a harbinger of this style, but the Renaissance Revival wasn't used for residences much before 1890. The Breakers, Cornelius Vanderbilt II's house in Newport, Rhode Island, was designed by Hunt and was completed in 1895. It was certainly the apotheosis of this style. Rich in its varied facade yet ordered in its superimposition of classical orders, the building exemplifies the grandiose assertion of the Italian pallazzo. The illustration shown is simpler in its details and more representative of most houses of this style.

As more and more Americans studied at the Ecole des Beaux-Arts and took the "grand tour" throughout Europe they saw palaces firsthand. Previously examples were only seen distilled in pattern books of the earlier Victorian era. After the First World War stone veneer construction was perfected and an increasing number of more modest examples of the style appeared. But it remained essentially a pretentious style. Lacking the charm of the Italianate or Italian Villa styles which were usually built of wood, these Renaissance Revivals always seem like a visiting grandee who never adapts to the American scene—who manages to keep his accent and clings to the security of his European manner. He is perhaps always a little bit suspect and more at ease in Palm Beach than in Northeast Harbor.

SECOND ITALIAN RENAISSANCE REVIVAL 1890–1930

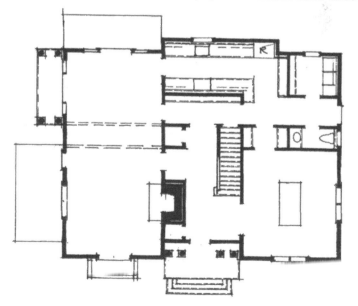

NEOCLASSICAL REVIVAL   1895–1950

For those who found the excessive monumentality of the Beaux-Arts classicism too ostentatious, the Neoclassical Revival was a viable alternative. Some of the smaller pavilions at the Columbian Exposition in 1893 inspired this revival. Though grandly assertive with its characteristic two-story classical portico—usually featuring the Ionic or Corinthian order—the style was generally restrained in its use of decorative details. The wall surfaces were smooth and plain and the moldings had little depth. Builders as well as architects, at least in the first quarter of the twentieth century, showed a concern for correctly proportioned classical orders.

Pilasters or possibly subtle quoins might appear at the corners of the building, but without great emphasis on shadow and depth. Symmetry was important and the portico usually dominated the central section of the facade. Blinds were not initially associated with this style.

Before 1920 hipped roofs were common and classical proportions were respected. From the mid-twenties on the general trend was toward side-gabled buildings and a much less fastidious replication of the classical orders.

When well done, these houses had a certain dignity, but the line between dignity and pomposity was tenuous at best. The Neoclassical Revival style was apt to exceed that subtle boundary and become pretentious. This became increasingly evident when the architectural details and proportions diverged from the classical standards. Some of the most grotesque, tasteless, and nouveau-riche buildings offered by speculative builders today are pale shadows of the Neoclassical Revival. One can often see the pretense carried to absurdity when a makeshift portico is slapped on the facade of a raised ranch or pseudo-colonial. Unfortunately it is not an uncommon sight.

NEOCLASSICAL REVIVAL 1895–1950

The redundant must be pared down, the superfluous dropped, the necessary itself reduced to its simplest expression, and then we shall find, whatever the organization may be, that beauty was waiting for us.

—Horatio Greenough, *Structure and Organization*, 1852

8. INDIGENOUS STYLES 1880–1930

The 1876 centennial exposition in Philadelphia triggered an interest in our nation's history and a sense of self-confidence and chauvinistic pride. No less than half of the most significant national patriotic and genealogical organizations were founded in the years between 1876 and 1896. Historical societies were formed in every old town. An American way of life—more "informal," "healthier," and "wholesome"—was conducive to an architecture that was subordinate to and showed deference to our regional landscape and varied terrain.

We did not have to import standards of design; we had developed the clipper ship and the yacht *America,* the trotting wagon, the Astor House (New York's first modern hotel), and the great Croton Reservoir. All were innovative and functional designs of exceptional utility and extraordinary beauty. Horatio Greenough (1805–1852) reminded us as early as 1843 that in art and esthetics "the first downward step was the introduction of the first inorganic, nonfunctional element, whether of shape or color."*

The Queen Anne and the Colonial Revival styles evolved in the 1880s and 1890s. They had derived from the more formal late Georgian and Federal styles but did not appeal to many Americans across the economic scale. Neither did the more pretentious European imports. Three distinct indigenous styles evolved, each in a different part of the country—one in the Northeast, one in the Midwest, and one in southern California—the Shingle style, the Prairie style, and the Craftsman style.

1) The Shingle style evolved in the Northeast as a cohesive, unified architectural mode inherently endowed with a sculpturally rich character that was distinctly American. While showing some influences from the English Queen Anne and the work of Norman Shaw (1831–1912) and his followers, Shingle houses demonstrated a mature style that drew from colonial precedent but with an entirely new sense of space, site, mass, and surface texture.

McKim, Mead & Bigelow designed a large house on Lloyd Neck on Long Island's north shore for Mrs. A. C. Alden in 1879. It predated Richardson's Stoughton house in Cambridge, Massachusetts, by three years and is the best candidate for the first landmark

---

*Greenough, Horatio, *American Architecture,* quoted in Hugh Morrison, *Early American Architecture* (New York: Oxford University Press, 1952; Dover, 1987).

Shingle style house. Vincent Scully said in his book *The Shingle Style* that this house "is one of the simplest and most coherent of any of the country houses built in America in the period before 1880."* Unfortunately the house was remodeled sometime in the early twentieth century and given a brick veneer. In popularity, the Shingle style was superseded by the revival styles around the turn of the century.

Fort Hill,
Mrs. A. C. Alden House, Lloyd Neck, Long Island, New York
by McKim, Mead & Bigelow, 1879–1880

The same firm, but with Stanford White now a partner, produced the Bell and the Goelet houses in Newport, Rhode Island, in 1882 and the Low house in Bristol, Rhode Island, four years later. All were landmark Shingle style houses. In the mid-1880s they turned their efforts away from the Shingle style and launched the Colonial Revival with their Appleton house in Lennox, Massachusetts, and the Taylor house in Newport, Rhode Island.

2) The Prairie style was developed by Frank Lloyd Wright and his fellow architects in Chicago at the turn of the century and Wright was its most accomplished proponent. Considered "too outré" by eastern architects who favored the historical or traditional styles, the Prairie School flourished until the end of the First World War; it has come to be appreciated in recent years as a style very much our own.

3) The Craftsman style evolved with the bungalow craze which began in California in the late 1890s. The word "bungalow" apparently derives from the Hindi word *bangala* meaning "of Bengal." The term was used to describe the one-story cottages with deep verandahs used by the British officers in India during the days of the Raj.

*Scully, Vincent J., Jr., *The Shingle Style* (New Haven, CT: Yale University Press, 1955).

Gustave Stickley published *The Craftsman* magazine from 1901 until 1916; it promoted houses that were "based upon the simplest and most direct principles of construction" and often featured the work of the Greene brothers. Charles S. and Henry M. Greene of Pasadena, California, were the first architects to echo the English Arts and Crafts movement in America and demonstrate the architectural potential of the Craftsman style. Some architectural writers call the Greene brothers' houses "Western Stick" or the "California style," but Craftsman seems a more appropriate term. Though lacking the sophistication of the Prairie style, the Craftsman interiors shared many characteristics—banks of windows, low profiles, open flowing floor plans, inglenooks, and the use of decorative banding with a predisposition for the horizontal.

Though they were submerged in the tide of reminiscent styles shortly before the First World War, all three of these styles, in their lack of borrowed or imported features, shone in their time as a beacon of rationality in a period of excess and disjointed eclecticism.

H. A. C. Taylor House,
Newport, Rhode Island,
by McKim, Mead & White,
1885–1886

Low House, Bristol, Rhode Island, by McKim Mead & White, 1886

SHINGLE 1880–1905

The term Shingle style (like "Stick style") was coined by Yale professor Vincent J. Scully, Jr., and was the title of his excellent book, *The Shingle Style,* published in 1955. He traced the development of this style from its evolution in the years following our centennial celebration in 1876. Drawing from various genetic forebears—the Queen Anne, the vernacular colonial styles, and the contemporaneous Colonial Revival—the style blossomed as something new and fresh. The Shingle style was not just a new set of superficial stylistic elements, but an organic style with a character derived from an open, fluid plan. The sculptural expression of inner volumes was given a cohesive unity by the naturally weathered shingle siding.

Lower courses—not just the exposed portion of the foundations but sometimes the entire first story—were often made of masonry. Smooth bricks with ⅛-inch mortar joints were commonly used in suburban settings, but often rustic stonework was employed in rural areas. Casement windows or double-hung sash windows were used and the sash was sometimes painted a cream color in contrast to a darker trim. Window trim was generally dark green or left natural. Unfortunately, many surviving shingle houses were highlighted with white in the Colonial Revival of the 1920s.

The architectural vocabulary used was vernacular but the actual compositions tended to be literate, articulate, and carefully edited. It is an architect's style when fully realized—ordered, disciplined, and comfortable with a sense of casual dignity. Many Colonial Revival houses were sided with shingles—but usually with corner boards and four-square massing and so do not really qualify as Shingle style.

Incidentally, Frank Lloyd Wright's Oak Park house that he built for himself in 1893 was Shingle style.

Frank Lloyd Wright's own house, 1893

SHINGLE 1880–1905

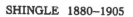

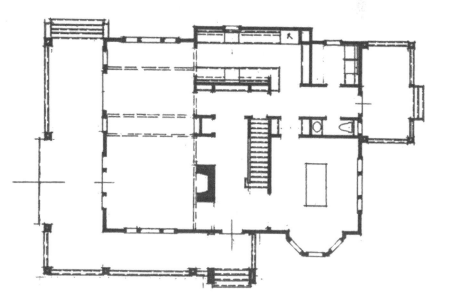

PRAIRIE   1900–1920

Less than a decade after he built his own Shingle style house in Oak Park, Frank Lloyd Wright developed a new and distinct regional style: the Prairie style. It featured open planning; shallow-pitched roofs with broad, sheltering overhangs; bands of casement windows, often with abstract patterns of stained glass; and a strong horizontal emphasis. The siding was usually stucco, either off-white or an earthy tone, with decorative banding that echoed the low horizon of the midwestern prairie. Porte cocheres and raised porches extending out from the main core of the house were typical features of the style.

Prairie houses grew in popularity during the first decade of the twentieth century and had many promoters. By 1910 there existed a definite vocabulary that defined a natural house that was sympathetic to the regional landscape. The school invented new decorative motifs and rejected all details that derived from European precedent.

Though popular in the Midwest, the Prairie style offended eastern establishment architects who were promoting the reminiscent styles, particularly the Colonial Revival. The 1918 jury for "A House for the Vacation Season," competition patronizingly awarded fourth prize for the single Prairie style submission with the comment that "it did not deserve all the cheap jokes passed upon it by its detractors." The jury also compared Prairie houses to railroad sleeping cars and warned that the occupants would have "no more privacy than a goldfish."

White Pine Series, 1918

PRAIRIE 1900–1920

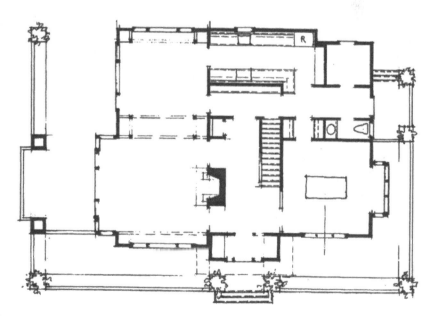

CRAFTSMAN 1900–1930

The Craftsman style originated in California in the 1890s. Gustave Stickley promoted the style in his magazine *The Craftsman* which he started in 1901. It is occasionally referred to in a derisive manner as the "Bungaloid style." Though the bungalow craze started in California as well, a bungalow is a building type and not a style.

The style is characterized by the rustic texture of the building materials, broad overhangs with exposed rafter tails at the eaves, and often extensive pergolas and trellises over the porches. Stone was never laid in a coursed ashlar pattern, but in a more random texture of rounded cobblestones. The lower portion of a wall was often battered or sloped near the ground. In the illustration, the porch columns are also tapered. The shingles on the second floor alternate with one course 2 inches "to the weather" and the next one 7½ inches exposed. Windows might be double-hung or casement, sometimes with different-sized window panes. The color and tone of the house derive from natural materials and an earth-toned stain applied to the wood. The Greene brothers' houses in southern California are perhaps the most elaborate examples of the style; they were the ultimate in refined craftsmanship.

The Craftsman style persisted throughout the 1920s in summer camps and modest suburbs throughout the country. Sears, Roebuck, Aladdin Redi-Cut, and other manufacturers of precut houses shipped Craftsman style houses wherever there were train tracks to carry them. People could simply pick a house out of a catalog and send away for it. The house came complete with doors, trim, and even plumbing. Everything, in fact, but the foundation, the well, and the septic system!

Typical bungalow

CRAFTSMAN 1900–1930

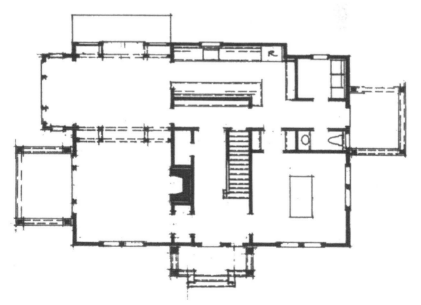

Among wealthy women, the real tastemakers, gardening supplanted elaborate costumes and decoration as a mark of feminine gentility and culture.

—Mark Alan Hewitt, *The Architect & the American Country House*, 1990

9. REMINISCENT STYLES   1880–1940

Much of our architecture after the Civil War reflected the enormous success of American entrepreneurs. While the architectural excesses were exemplified by the apotheosis of the Queen Anne style—the Carson house in Eureka, California—and the palatial mansions of the Gilded Age, these excesses produced two basic responses. One was a search for the good life in a rural setting; the other was a step backwards into a simpler age for the character of American houses. The Arts and Crafts movement in England had its counterpart here in the Shingle style, the Prairie style, and the Craftsman style, all of which evolved as a reaction against the excessive eclecticism of the late nineteenth century. Whether the houses were of a formal traditional style or an interpretation of the more regional vernacular styles, the early decades of this century nurtured a new American way of living, much less formal than the English. There was a search for a comfortable rural life on farms—at least on weekends and during the summer months—where gardening and sports became a part of our lives.

In the period from 1910 to 1929—a time of prodigious house building—the Colonial Revival styles prevailed. The House and Garden movement flourished and the palatial palaces of the 1890s were viewed by most taste-makers as vulgar, pretentious, and ostentatious. The established class had money, leisure, and an interest in the good life. Life was less restricted—sports, riding, tennis, and golf included women—and houses became more a part of the landscape rather than an assertion of dominance over it. The Country Club founded in Brookline, Massachusetts, in 1882 was the first of many golf and tennis clubs. Corinthian yacht clubs (where owners handled their own boats rather than having professional crews) sprang up along the Atlantic coast, and the Garden Club of America was founded in 1913.

House and Garden, Country Life in America, House Beautiful, The Craftsman, and the *White Pine Series of Architectural Monographs* were popular periodicals of the day. The White Pine Series sponsored a number of architectural competitions for house designs and the jury always included such distinguished residential architects as William Delano, Harrie Lindeberg, and Cass Gilbert. It is interesting, and I think revealing, to examine the attitudes of these juries around the time of the First World War. In praising the submissions in 1916, the jury admired "simple, direct, and logical solutions," complimented "artistic skill" combined with "practical good sense," and encouraged "fitness of purpose" and "direct sound construction." "A good common sense livable house" should be "simple and dignified," "simple" but "full of charm." "A wise use of simple materials and simple forms is another sign of good taste which is rapidly coming into favor." "The exterior is so quiet and so simple as to have the charm that goes with all restrained work."

In commenting on American houses in 1918, the jury said, "we have completely avoided the pit falls of over-loaded ornament and the straining after something new, which has injured the architecture of both France and England and absolutely vulgarized any shred of good taste in Germany." Though admittedly "doing the most restrained and most conservative work," they emphasized that "if we do not want the architectural tree to die of dry-rot, we should welcome these alien grafts, however wild and wanton their growth or however strange their bloom." In doing so they awarded fourth prize in 1918 for a vacation house to a Prairie style design cribbed from Frank Lloyd Wright's Allen House, built in Wichita, Kansas, in 1917. (See the illustration on page 112.)

Mark Alan Hewitt, in his excellent book *The Architect & the American Country House*, said that it is time that these reminiscent houses "again be regarded as they were by the critics in their day, as key examples of a building type that contributed uniquely to modern American architecture."* The architects of these houses found in simple regional architecture prototypes for the twentieth century. Even the rural vernacular styles of the English Cotswolds and countryside of Normandy were more comfortably at home on our shores than were Greek and Roman temples, Oriental harems, or spaceships from another galaxy. Why? Because they were of the land and were simple and direct vernacular solutions to similar kinds of architectural problems.

Good sound organization of space, an understanding of site planning, and "simple, direct, and logical solutions" are independent of style. The admonishments of the White Pine jurists are as appropriate today as they were seventy-five years ago. It doesn't mean that we must copy specific details or imitate historical styles, but there is

---

*Hewitt, Mark Alan, *The Architect & the American Country House* (New Haven, CT: Yale University Press, 1990).

much to be learned by studying the works of the architects who responded to the conservative domestic programs of their clients and found inspiration in the unpretentious and even modest rural structures both here and abroad.

Country Life in America *first appeared in 1901 and continued as a popular magazine into World War II—its last issue was published in 1942. It stressed a theme of a genteel rural life.*

The August 1925 issue featured The Arthur E. Newbold estate on Philadelphia's "Main Line" by Mellor, Meigs & Howe, which epitomized the French Rural style—often called Manoir or Normandy Farmhouse.

EARLY COLONIAL REVIVAL 1885–1915

The centennial exposition in Philadelphia in 1876 stimulated a chauvinistic pride in our country. Though the Queen Anne style and the Shingle style both were popular in the 1880s, architects and pattern books encouraged a retrospective view of our late Georgian and Federal styles. These neo-Georgian and Adamesque revivals were much larger buildings than their prototypes. Their designs were freely drawn from or inspired by their late eighteenth-century predecessors and were only reminiscent of the earlier styles. Windows were generally larger than in the originals and usually had divided lights only on the upper sash. No actual Colonial or Federal house ever used paired windows; their appearance is usually an instant clue to the age of the house. Great liberties were also taken with proportions and scale.

In 1877 Charles Follen McKim and his partner William Rutherford Mead made a "colonial" tour through New England with Stanford White who was soon to become their partner. They were looking for inspiration from our American architectural heritage. Their design for the Misses Appleton house in Lennox, Massachusetts, in 1883–1884 was perhaps the first major Colonial Revival house. The Taylor house, another early example of the style, was also built by them in Newport in 1885–1886.

The Early Colonial Revival borrowed eighteenth-century details and applied them to simplified Queen Anne houses. By the early 1900s, however, architects began to produce more "authentic" houses in the Colonial styles. Sometimes it is hard to tell the difference but for the predilection for paired windows and the ubiquitous side porch on Colonial Revival houses. The opening of restored Williamsburg in the 1930s gave a tremendous impetus to the revival of Southern Colonial styles and the "center hall colonial." What real estate people call "colonial" is, for the most part, a style from the early nineteenth century. The ubiquitous, stark-white house with green or black louvered blinds was typical of the Greek Revival style and did not appear until the 1820s.

EARLY COLONIAL REVIVAL 1885–1915

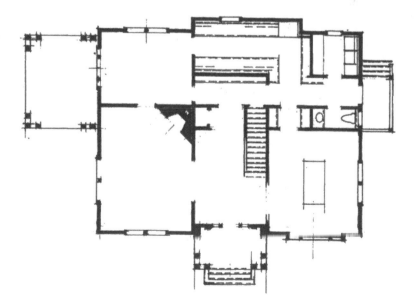

DUTCH COLONIAL   1890–1930

What is generally called Dutch Colonial is a house with a gambrel roof where one or both of the lower slopes flares at the eaves in a gentle curve. Though the gambrel roof was used in New England from the earliest days, the upper roof pitch is longer and steeper than the Dutch prototype. The Dutch made the lower portion of the roof longer and with a shallower pitch.

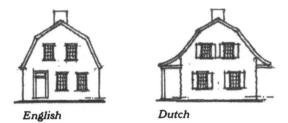

English   *Dutch*

With the possible exception of Dutch tiles around the fireplace openings, most details of the Dutch Colonial Revival follow the standard Colonial Revival patterns and are indistinguishable from them. Shutters with a decorative hole instead of louvered blinds were fairly common. The hole was apt to be cut in the shape of a half-moon, a pine tree, or a bell. Dormers either were separate roof structures or were a continuous element for nearly the full length of the building.

It is curious that the prototypes of the Dutch Colonial Revival were built throughout the Hudson River Valley and New Jersey but were not replicas of any house built in Holland. Scholars simply do not agree whether the characteristic roof of this Revival style was an adaptation of a Flemish farmhouse or was an original type developed here as an amalgamation of several colonial building patterns borrowed from the English.

Aymar Embury II (1880–1966) was a New York architect who did much to promote the style after 1910. He attempted to create a more "authentic" version of a colonial house than one would find in a Sears, Roebuck and Company or an Aladdin Redi-Cut catalog. The actual stepped-gabled, brick buildings of New Netherland were never revived in a twentieth-century adaptation of the style.

DUTCH COLONIAL 1890–1930

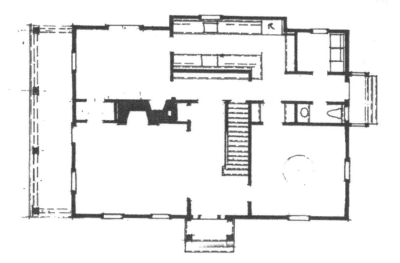

ELIZABETHAN   1910–1940

Next to Colonial Revival, the term Tudor is used to describe a greater range of house types than any other. In real-estate parlance, almost any front-gabled house with a steep roof and a large chimney is called Tudor. Elizabethan is used to describe half-timbered houses that derive more from the cottage or farmhouse than from the mansion.

The cross-gables, steeply pitched roofs, large chimney stacks with clustered flues or even spiral designs, all help identify the style. Tall windows with mullions and transoms framing casements with leaded glass are also typical features. The lower story is often brick and the floor framing of the second floor is projected out on the exterior a foot or so as it was in our early New England colonial houses. The two styles actually share the same architectural genes. The half-timbered effect—whether real or suggested by applied boards—confirms the style. Many Americans visited Stratford-upon-Avon and saw Anne Hathaway's cottage which was the apotheosis of the Elizabethan cottage, complete with thatched roof.

The Elizabethan style became very popular after the First World War and continued to be built through the Depression years. Though it went into eclipse in the forties, it resurged in the seventies and eighties in a kind of pseudo-style. Called Neo-Tudor, its fake half-timbering is never convincing and has more of the quality of a stage set than a real house. I have never understood why anyone would want to live in a stage set.

Anne Hathaway's Cottage

ELIZABETHAN 1910–1940

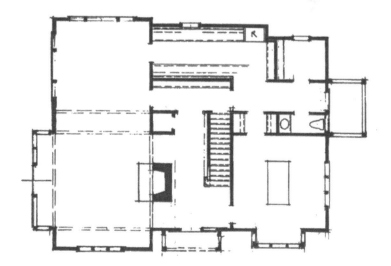

SPANISH MISSION   1890–1920

Just as the East was looking to its colonial past for architectural precedent and Colonial Revival work proliferated, the Southwest looked to the Spanish architecture of its colonial era for inspiration. The Spanish Mission churches with their Baroque parapeted gables and fanciful wall dormers were the impetus for the Mission style. The dominant curved parapet specifically identifies this style. Red tile roofs, projecting eaves with exposed rafter ends, and open porches with square or rectangular piers are all typical characteristics.

The Mission style started in California but soon spread when the Santa Fe and Southern Pacific Railroad adopted the style for their stations and resort hotels. It gradually spread east and crops up in surprising places. For example, the railway station and adjoining commercial buildings in Ridgewood, New Jersey, are all Spanish Mission style with green tile roofs. After the Panama-California Exposition in San Diego in 1915, which featured the Spanish Colonial architecture, the Spanish Colonial Revival gained further impetus and the Spanish Mission style became simply one of many eclectic styles that derived from original Spanish colonial precedents.

It is important to note that the term Spanish Mission should not be confused with the mission furniture popularized by Gustave Stickley in his *Craftsman* magazine in the early 1900s. Mission furniture was an Arts and Crafts style promoted by artisans and manufacturers who "had a mission" to simplify and improve furniture design. Mission furniture might well be called "craftsman" as it complemented the architectural design of the Craftsman and Prairie styles.

Typical mission church c. 1700

SPANISH MISSION 1890–1920

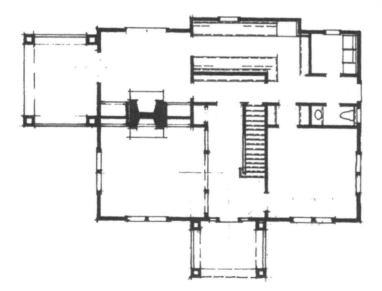

PUEBLO   1900–1990s

J. C. Schweinfurth's Hacienda del Pozo de Verona in Pleasanton, California, designed for Phoebe Apperson Hearst in 1898 was the first major residential commission designed in the Pueblo style. The single most important indicator of the style is the projection of roof beams a foot or so out from the adobe wall. They are called *vigas*.

The prototype for the Pueblo style was the Governor's Palace built in Sante Fe, New Mexico, in 1609 (see page 30). It was a blending of the local Indian building techniques with Spanish planning and details. A one-story adobe structure about 800 feet long, it had a covered porch, called a *portales*, extending almost the entire length of the building. The porch roof was a wood framework supported by wooden posts capped with bracket capitals (no arches, domes, or vaults). The patio side faces a lush garden—a Spanish contribution to this composite style.

Indian pueblos were multistoried structures made of sun-dried clay. The flat roofs were framed with straight poles. Smaller saplings were laid crosswise to the poles, and the entire framework of the roof encased in clay. If the *vigas* were prominent features so were the rainwater spouts, called *canales*, which also projected from the building and became another identifying feature. The Indians who inhabited these structures composed stable agricultural tribes who built pueblos as early as the ninth century. San Geronimo near Taos, New Mexico, was built about 1540. The Indians used the inner rooms to store supplies. Originally there were no doors at the lower level and people climbed ladders for access to the upper level. With the ladders removed, the buildings became effective forts with ample supplies to resist attacks.

The Pueblo style proliferated in the 1920s and 1930s and is still common in the Southwest. It seems a much more appropriate style than the pseudo-Mediterranean pallazzos that are promoted by many developers in that area.

Vigas   *Canales*

PUEBLO 1900–1990s

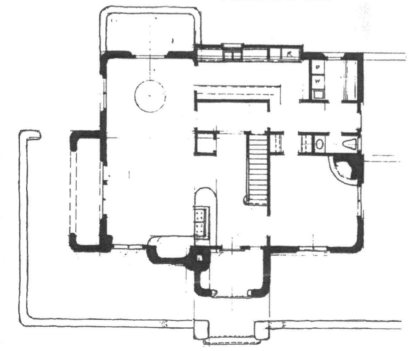

SPANISH COLONIAL REVIVAL   1915–1940

The 1915 Panama-California Exposition in San Diego was designed by Bertram Grosvenor Goodhue (1869–1924), an influential proponent of Spanish Colonial architecture adapted to the twentieth century. The climate and cultural heritage made the style eminently suited to the Southwest—California, Arizona, New Mexico, Texas, and even Florida.

The red tile roofs, the simple forms subtly embellished at doorways, and the ornamental ironwork serving as protective barriers over windows were common details. The House & Garden movement in the East, which encouraged the concept of the house as a part of its own landscaped domain, had its counterpart in the Southwest. The simplicity of a Spanish courtyard with shade trees, hanging baskets, and flowering shrubs can hardly be surpassed.

Not all Spanish Colonial Revival houses managed to recreate the romantic character of a true hacienda. In too many instances suburban houses of no architectural distinction were identified as "Spanish" by the use of tile roofs, stucco walls, heavy wooden doors, and perhaps some ornamental ironwork. Very popular in the 1920s and 1930s, the style's popularity declined after the Second World War.

The most lasting legacy of the Spanish Colonial Revival as a national type was the one-story house which we know as the ranch house. Its characteristic U-shaped floor plan with a protected patio in the courtyard derives from the California *ranchos* of the 1830s.

Ranch house c. 1835

SPANISH COLONIAL REVIVAL 1915–1940

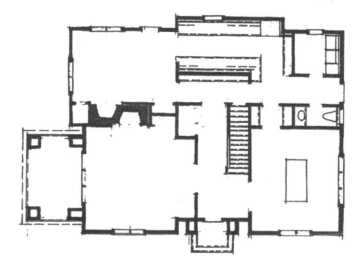

MONTEREY   1925–1955

More than ten years before gold was discovered at Sutter's Mill, California, Yankee merchants were sailing around Cape Horn and trading with the Spanish along the southern Pacific coast. In 1821 the Mexican government started granting huge tracts of land to Spanish entrepreneurs to encourage private ranching. The 1830s and 1840s was a prosperous era and there was a lively trade in hides and tallow. Monterey, Santa Barbara, and San Diego became important ports (San Francisco not until 1849).

Thomas Larkin, a Boston merchant, built a house for himself in Monterey in 1837 which blended the basic two-story New England colonial house with Spanish adobe construction. Virtually all previous Spanish colonial houses were one story. This innovation combined with double-height roofed *corredors* (porches) around the structure to create a new style. The gently sloped roof was often covered with wood shingles instead of tile and served to protect the adobe walls—another innovation in the Spanish territory.

Interior fireplaces, kitchens, and glazed windows were all new features in the California landscape. Though redwood was available for house construction, people continued to build with adobe. They found that it was much cooler during the summer, and in the colder months the thick walls absorbed heat during the day and slowly radiated it during the night. This was the most fundamental principle of passive solar heating at work.

In the 1920s the compulsive search for colonial precedent led to a revival of the Monterey style. Interpretations of the Monterey style house can now be found in every part of the country.

Thomas Larkin House, Monterey, California, 1837

MONTEREY 1925–1955

FRENCH RURAL   1915–1940

Americans who studied at the Ecole des Beaux-Arts in the nine-teenth century studied classical architecture—particularly the gran-diose classicism associated with the school. As the revival styles caught on here prior to the First World War, the rural vernacular architecture of the French countryside became an important in-spiration for our residential architecture. The steeply pitched hip roof with subtly flared curves at the eaves, the circular stair towers, and the substantial but uncoursed stonework had tremendous ap-peal to Americans. Many of our soldiers came back from the war with an appreciation of the rural beauty of France. Young artists, writers, and architects went to France in the twenties and our love affair with France continued. H. D. Eberlein's *Small Manor Houses and Farmsteads in France* published in 1926 and Samuel Cham-berlain's *Domestic Architecture of Rural France* in 1928 were popu-lar resources for residential architects.

Philadelphia was particularly receptive to these rural French houses. Normandy Village in Chestnut Hill and the work of Mellor, Meigs & Howe on the Main Line were particularly important. Arthur Meig's idyllic farm complex for Arthur E. Newbold, Jr., in Laverock appeared on the cover of *Country Life in America* in 1925 and captured the essence of the movement (see page 119).

In our desire to identify house styles with a particular time and place which we feel express feelings about ourselves, we use names like "Normandy farmhouse," "French Provincial" (although that term has come to imply something pretty vulgar in recent years), or, for the anglophile, the "Cotswold cottage." One or two small details can suggest one style over another when in fact the basic houses are quite similar. All are basically forms of a comfortable country style.

FRENCH RURAL 1915–1940

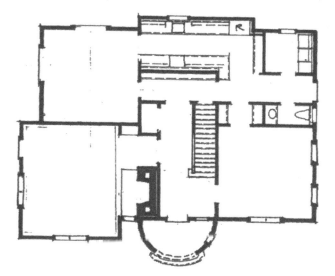

Education has been described as the process of learning to defend oneself against unnecessary information. Since there is no such thing in architecture as unnecessary information, all architects automatically consider themselves as educated to the highest degree. This is a comforting delusion, but has been known to lead to impressive fiascoes.

—Eugene Raskin, *Architecture and People,* 1974

10. THE MODERN MOVEMENT 1920–1960

The essence of modern architecture is rationalism. Spaces are planned to suit their functions and are defined by structural systems that exploit the efficiency of contemporary materials and innovative building techniques. Logic precludes such artificial dictums as formal symmetry and extraneous ornament that, as professor Eugene Raskin once said, "chattered at us in their neoclassical jargon." New shapes, plain surfaces, and unfamiliar structures evolved not just as a new aesthetic but also as simple common sense.

Le Corbusier's (1887–1965) description of the house as a "machine for living in" captured the essence of the Modern aesthetic in Europe. His book *Vers Une Architecture* was first published in Paris in 1923 and translated into English in 1927. He articulated the view of the post–World War I European architect. The Bauhaus, founded in Weimer, Germany, in 1919, was the academy of this new architecture. It moved to Dessau, Germany, in 1926 and flourished as the High School for Creative Art under Walter Gropius until 1928 and later under Mies van der Rohe (1886–1969). When Hitler came to power in 1934, Gropius emigrated to England. Three years later he moved to Cambridge, Massachusetts, where he became head of the School of Design at Harvard. Numerous disciples came to America with him—among them Marcel Breuer, who stayed to practice in the East, and Mies who became head of the Illinois Institute of Technology. All these architects embraced a machine aesthetic which, while appropriate for commercial and corporate programs, seemed—in its pure form—antithetical to residential design. These Internationalists rejected all applied ornament, scorned any reference in form or detail to historic or traditional styles, and promoted mass-produced factory components as the essence of the new aesthetic. I remember in the late fifties hearing Boston architect Serge Chermayeff quip in his terse British intonation that "Mies van der Rohe discovered marble, steel, and glass back in 1920 and he's been polishing the hell out of them ever since!"

What came to be recognized as "Modern" was a rather stark new style. But its underlying logic was not always understood. Stripped-down buildings had a superficial modern appearance but were in fact often inefficiently planned and badly constructed. A building is bad not because it looks "too modern" but because it is perhaps not modern enough. If an architect fails to consider the psychological needs of the client as well as the physical needs, his or her buildings can never be truly functional.

A utilitarian structure may work well—a chicken coop, a gas station, or an airplane hangar, for example, are efficient—but it can't be considered architecture, certainly not good architecture, unless it transcends its physical functions and encompasses the needs of the psyche as well. If, for example, people are rarely taller than 6 feet, why have ceilings any higher than 6 feet 6 inches? That is high enough to accommodate anyone but a member of the New York Knicks. The answer, of course, is that we need breathing room. We would feel claustrophobic in such a compressed space. In the same way, we expect floors to be level, doors and windows to be vertical, and spaces to be proportioned to an innate sense of scale that is part of our very nature. Also, most of us crave some kind of architectural enrichment. In *The Comfortable House,* Alan Gowans observed that "any and all buildings above the utilitarian level have style (whether high style, popular/commercial, vernacular or vestigial). Style, and the sense of ornament that is an integral part of it, seems to fulfill an intrinsic human need. Repressed, that need comes out in vulgarized forms."* One look at an occupied dormitory room on any college campus and you will see the gratification of that human need fulfilled with gusto.

Intended as a panacea for a decadent society in Germany after the First World War, Modern architecture of the European variety never became popular here for residential design. It is ironic that the machine aesthetic became an elitist avant-garde architecture among sophisticated urbanites for weekend retreats and was never embraced by the majority of American homeowners. The notion of "starting from zero" was too cerebral for most Americans and the Modernists' reasons for rejecting all precedent in our houses was patently absurd. The International style was usually tempered somewhat in American applications—the existence of a pure, geometrically sculptural phenomenon that was at odds with its environment is fortunately rare in this country. Such houses are usually an affront to nature and the community, much like a rude and assertive boor who enjoys making a spectacle of himself wherever he goes or a religious fanatic with a missionary zeal.

In the celebration of the machine—of man's dominance over nature—there is an inherent arrogance. Glass boxes can be heated

*Gowans, Alan, *The Comfortable House* (Cambridge, MA: MIT Press, 1986).

and cooled by mechanical means (technology), but usually at great expense. There are more inventive ways of evolving a design that is at the same time more compatible with its surroundings — both natural and man-made (native ingenuity). A more organic approach to architecture is just as modern but not as strictly ideological in its rejection of all traditional conventions. The Bauhaus architecture, as it came to be promoted here, failed to encompass a broad enough range of human needs and was eventually superseded by a more inclusive approach to architectural design. Mies van der Rohe's epithet "Less is more" became scorned in the 1960s as "Less is a bore" even by many former believers, and Postmodernism appeared on the scene.

MODERNE   1920–1940

Architectural programs in the modern age required new approaches to basic design. The elevator and the skyscraper went hand in hand; so did the automobile and the motor lodge, and the infinite changes in our house design with the advent of washing machines, dishwashers, telephones, and vacuum cleaners. The publication of Frank Lloyd Wright's houses in Europe in 1910 started the movement toward an international sharing of architectural ideas. Charles Rennie Macintosh in Scotland; Charles F. A. Voysey in England; Henri van deVelde in Belgium; Peter Behrens and J. M. Olbrich in Germany; Adolph Loos in Austria; H. P. Berlage and J. J. P. Oud in Holland; and Augueste Perret and Tony Garnier in France all searched for solutions to new architectural problems and for ways to use new materials and new methods of production in the years before the First World War.

In the years after the war architects saw a chance to contribute to a new and better world. True modern architecture involved a new way of thinking which meant rejecting most conventional design standards.

New buildings devoid of ornament, with plain surfaces and the latest in plate-glass windows, often had the appearance of modernity but were frequently just stripped-down versions of old building types. More often than not they were as badly planned and as inefficient as the old.

Moderne—or, in its more disparaging term, Modernistic—was really a case of superficial styling. Buildings were pseudo-modern, simply dressed in a new set of clothes. I don't mean to denigrate the Moderne style, but simply streamlining buildings, adding glass block, featuring lally columns and maybe a wraparound window or two is really more style than substance. At least most of the time.

Art Deco is sometimes called Modernistic and can be confused with Moderne. Actually it is a style of ornamant (like Eastlake in the late nineteenth century) which was popular in the 1920s and 1930s for office buildings, movie theaters, and apartment houses. It is easy to identify by its frets, zigzags, chevrons, and angular, stylized floral motifs usually set in low relief in decorative panels. The style was virtually never used in houses.

MODERNE 1920-1940

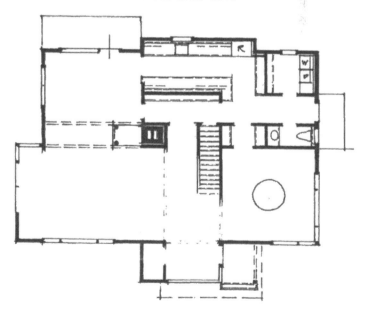

INTERNATIONAL STYLE   1930–1990s

The term International style was coined in 1932 when H. R. Hitchcock and Philip Johnson organized an exhibit of modern architecture at the Museum of Modern Art in New York. Their book, *The International Style: Architecture Since 1922*, was published as a corollary to the exhibit. Both had a tremendous influence on the course of modern architecture in America.

There were three basic attributes of the style: 1) The structure changed from load-bearing walls to a skeletal frame with an exterior skin (a thin curtain wall of glass and insulated panels) which became a barrier to the elements but not part of the structural system. Volume replaced mass as the main design consideration. 2) The exterior of a building should express the nature of the inner structural core and the spaces that structure defined. The building's character was consequently not determined by such artificial conventions as axial symmetry and ornament. 3) Any and all decoration or ornament was omitted from the design. Even window and door surrounds were as inconspicuous as possible; surfaces were plain and pure white.

Neither Gill's Dodge House (1914–1916) nor Schindler's Lovell House (1922–1926) on pages 14 and 15 could be considered International style. The first was more concerned with the massing of separate forms, and the second was too sculptural in its celebration of cantilevered construction. Both were modern, but neither was ideological enough to be called International. In contrast, Le Corbusier's Villa Savoye (1928–1930) near Paris was featured in the MOMA exhibit. It captured all of the characteristics of the International style and remains undoubtedly the quintessential example of the style.

Villa Savoye, 1929

INTERNATIONAL 1930–1990s

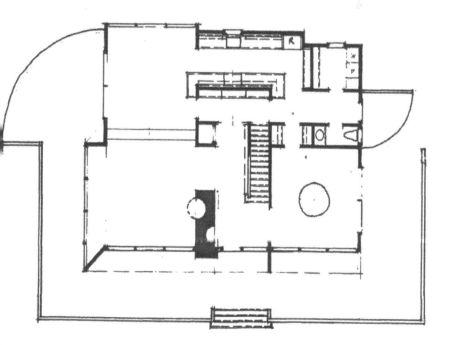

WRIGHTIAN   1940–1960

Frank Lloyd Wright was almost seventy in 1936 when he designed Fallingwater. His first so-called "Usonian" house for the Jacobs family near Madison, Wisconsin, was finished the following year (see page 17). His commissions had been sporadic during the twenties but the Administration Building for the Johnson Wax Company in Racine, Wisconsin, as well as Wingspread, a house for Mr. Johnson, both in 1937, sparked a whole new career which flourished undiminished until his death in 1959 at the age of ninety-two. His energy and fresh ideas assured his place in the development of modern architecture even had these later buildings been his first commissions.

The houses Wright designed in the forties and fifties, which numbered no less than 150, incorporated natural materials in a way that made his houses an integral part of the site. He almost invariably used coursed stone or brick, tall French doors, flat or shallow-pitched roofs, often with a dentilled fascia, and extensive parapeted railings built up of overlapping boards. Wright introduced mitered glass at exterior corners and avoided contained spaces. He always stressed that he "destroyed the box" by the use of cantilevered construction where corner posts were structurally unnecessary; this allowed a sense of spatial freedom. He developed designs with strong geometric shapes and explored the design possibilities of hexagons (using a thirty/sixty degree triangle) and circular forms.

Wright inspired many young architects and his legacy lives on. Unfortunately, too many of his followers produced mannered designs that only superficially reflected his work. "Wrightian" should never really be considered a style; rather it should be thought of as a way of building. Wright used the term "organic" to describe his work. It defies precise definition—a quality which is at the heart of all great art. And the majority of Wright's houses are indeed works of art.

"What we call organic architecture is no mere aesthetic nor cult nor fashion but an actual movement based on a profound idea of a new integrity of human life wherein art, religion, and science are one: form and function seem as one, of such is democracy."—FLW, 1953

WRIGHTIAN 1940–1960

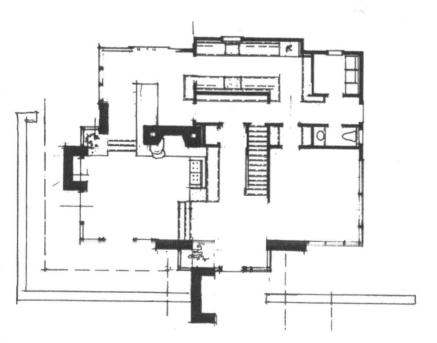

146

POPULAR HOUSE STYLES   1945–1990s
CONTEMPORARY AND TRADITIONAL

Building boomed after the Second World War. Generally developers built small Cape Cods, ranch houses, or modest two-story cottages. There was no particular concern for style and there were few pretentious houses. Even custom builders used the same basic layouts— maybe a little larger all around but still quite spartan compared to the luxurious accommodations which have been standard since the early 1980s.

The four-square and the bungalow, which met the housing needs of middle America from the turn of the century to the Depression years, were abandoned in favor of basic English colonial styles and ranch houses evolved from Spanish prototypes. All designs tended to be based on American precedents. The economic depression of the 1930s and the ideology of modern architecture had both made sufficient impact on Americans before the war to obviate the need for fancy details. These postwar houses were termed "Minimal Traditional."*

By the early 1950s, new designs began to appear: the split-level; the raised ranch; variations on Williamsburg colonials, "center hall colonials," and garrison colonials and the two-story Contemporary that owed some of its character to the Prairie style and to the detailing of the single-story ranch house. Though modern amenities were certainly incorporated into the new houses, the modern styles imported from Europe were considered suspect by most Americans. Architects generally embraced the rationale of modern architecture and favored so-called Contemporaries, while builders tended to be wary and stuck to more reminiscent designs. Californians were perhaps the exception; they always seemed open to new ideas.

Today, builders continue to offer what they perceive the public wants: anything associated with the old rather than the new. It does not seem to matter how inept the planning or how gross the details as long as the house has divided lights in the windows, French doors instead of sliders, and a prominently pitched roof. And, of course, the more molding on the inside the better. Perhaps this is a desire for the accoutrements of stability and permanence in a rootless

*McAlester, Virginia and Lee, *A Field Guide to American Houses* (New York: Knopf, 1984/89).

society. One thing, however, is certain: the general public has repudiated the International style in favor of something homier and more livable.

Builders are quick to reflect the taste of the times, and a hodgepodge of historic eclecticism prevails today. Architects, on the other hand, have generally been less responsive to the public's predilection for reminiscent architecture and have persisted in promoting experimental and eccentric designs. Postmodernism's professed "contexturalism" and "inclusivism" are largely illusionary. A cutout of a column stuck on the facade of a house does not make it compatible with a 1840 Greek Revival house next door. Perhaps a synthesis of the two positions holds more promise. Architects are often perceived as too contemporary or too Postmodern with proper justification in many instances—too much style and not enough content.

As this book is a guide to American house styles, what follows is a collection of the principal popular styles offered by builders and developers since the end of the Second World War, as well as some that have been favored by architects. All the houses shown have the same floor plan as the ones in the previous chapters, but here a breezeway and garage are also included.

As an architect I naturally have my own credo. The comments and observations with respect to the following examples are strictly personal. They reflect my bias for styles that are unpretentious and generally show a deference for regional architecture, the

Ground floor plan

locale, and natural surroundings. I purposely omit the term "Contemporary" as a distinct style because it is too imprecise to mean anything. It has negative connotations for some and positive images for others when in fact there is probably more common ground between the two than one would initially expect.

"Regional" is a term that might be used more. To me it implies a respect for regional character and vernacular conventions which can spark creative architectural designs that are new and fresh and responsive to the program requirements of a client and yet complement the existing community and terrain.

MINIMAL TRADITIONAL 1935–1950

A compromise style of the Depression years. Usually one story or one-and-a-half stories, multigabled with little or no decorative details. Often suggestive of the Tudor houses of the 1920s with a front facing gable and a fairly large chimney but with a much shallower roof pitch.

Ranch   Split-Level

RANCH and SPLIT-LEVEL 1950–1965

These are not really styles; they are building types and can appear in any number of costumes. So prevalent during the 1950s and early 1960s, they cannot be omitted from this guide. Most have fixed blinds (that probably could not even cover the window), fancy porch posts or wrought-iron supports, and contrasting brick veneer on the front.

NEO-COLONIAL REVIVAL 1950–1970s

The real-estate developers' staple, they are invariably pale reflections of the original prototypes. Roof pitches are usually too low and windows badly proportioned. Unlike the Colonial Revival houses of the 1920s, here there is no reverence for the past. With aluminum siding, fixed vinyl blinds, and a little brick veneer to dress up the entrance side, they are the quintessential "phony colonies."

WILLIAMSBURG COLONIAL 1950 1990s

Colonial Williamsburg opened in the early 1930s and this one-and-a-half-story Southern Colonial has been popular ever since. With symmetrical facades and fairly steeply pitched roofs with dormers, these houses are usually of either clapboard or brick.

MIESIAN 1950–1965 (rare)
Ludwig Mies van der Rohe (1886–1969) espoused the dictum that "Less is more" and designed elegantly spartan buildings. The Seagram Building in New York (1954–58) is his most famous work. Unconcerned with climate, site, and natural forces, some of his admirers designed houses using his sense of modular steel frame construction. Philip Johnson was his most devoted follower and his famous 1949 Glass House in New Canaan, Connecticut, is the most successful example of this style.

BRUTALISM 1960–1980 (even rarer than Miesian)
Though "brutal" in its rugged and frank use of exposed poured concrete, brickwork inside and out, and massive sense of scale, the name supposedly derives from British architect Peter "Brutus" Smithson who was an early proponent of the style. Rarely seen in houses, the Boston City Hall by Kallman, McKinnell & Knowles (1961–68) is the best example of the style.

BUILDER'S CONTEMPORARY 1960–1985

Builders adopted the simplified details and massing of architects' contemporary designs. Vertical siding or clapboards with natural stains, large windows, and numerous skylights were all characteristic of the style. Roofs were usually hipped or hipped in combination with low-pitched gables.

MANSARD 1960–1990s

The modern builder's interpretation of the French roof was another cliché that caught on in the 1960s and is still fairly common. It bears little resemblance to the Second Empire style of the 1870s. Smooth stucco walls with decorative quoins, double front doors, and arched windows with louvered blinds are typical features of this style.

SUPERMANNERIST 1960–1970s

An exuberant Postmodern style characterized by eccentric massing, whimsical fenestration, and decorated with flamboyant colors and bold graphics. House numbers, for example, might be boldly featured. The facades often resemble huge advertising displays.

NEO-SHINGLE 1960–1980s

An unfortunate term given to the first of the so-called Postmodern variations, these architect-designed houses derived from vernacular prototypes and often used shingles. Though sometimes crisp and unselfconscious, they were more often obtuse and perversely iconoclastic, disdaining convention in favor of mannered eccentricity.

BUILDER'S SHED 1965–1980s

The multidirectional shed roof—a vernacular form—was widely used by architects in the 1960s and was soon imitated by builders across the country. Diagonal siding with brown stain and aluminum sliding windows were typical. Usually there was no projecting overhang or fascia at the eaves and the massing was often complex.

POSTMODERN 1960s–1990s

The term applies to any of the architect-designed houses that incorporate details and features from a checklist of trendy clichés. Stylized classical references and vernacular buildings blend in an amalgamation of affectation. Pastel colors, stripes, and eccentricity characterize the style.

NEO-CLASSICAL REVIVAL 1965–1990s
Neo-Neoclassical Revival would be a better term. The two-story portico is the key feature of this style. The disfigured classical orders are inept reflections of the early nineteenth century and turn-of-the-century prototypes. It is sad to see classical orders reduced to such pathetic imitations.

NEO-TUDOR 1965–1990s
"Tudor" is usually applied to almost any front-gabled house with a steeply pitched roof, a prominent chimney, and fake half-timbered boards. These houses are rarely built of stone as the more "authentic" Tudors were in the 1920s. Mock-Tudor or Mock-'bethan would perhaps be more appropriate terms.

NEO-MEDITERRANEAN 1970–1990s
The term applies to almost any vaguely Spanish or Italian Renaissance house with a red tile roof (usually simulated), stuccoed walls, some round arched windows and doors, and a fancy front door. Common in the former Spanish territories of California, the Southwest, and Florida, they are inappropriately built throughout the country.

NEO-FRENCH ECLECTIC 1975–1990s
The revival of various "traditional" styles in the 1970s heralded a rejection of modern architecture and a search for a more pretentious old-house look. The segmented arches over the windows and doors and the decorative quoins are characteristics of this style. Front doors are apt to be elaborately embellished with classical motifs.

NOUVEAU TRADITIONAL 1980s–1990s

*No style has yet evolved that so grossly and blatantly expresses the os-
tentatious and pretentious excesses of an era than these eclectic excres-
cences that have become the staple of "upscale" developers.*

DECONSTRUCTIONIST 1980s–1990s

*A sort of Post-Postmodernism, these designs are novel, quirky, and per-
versely eccentric. On the level of civil liberties, I am glad we are permit-
ted to express ourselves in public, but I would prefer that free speech
was verbal rather than quite so permanent—even in California where
the style originated.*

NEO-VICTORIAN 1980–1990s
Renewed interest in Queen Anne houses of the late nineteenth century has launched the usual surge of imitations. Some of the excesses of the 1980s found expression in the revival of elaborate spindlework, scrolls and brackets, and the architectural vocabulary of the late Victorian era.

AMERICAN VERNACULAR REVIVAL 1980–1990s
Unpretentious regional architecture can be an excellent starting point for new designs for our era. Good planning can comfortably complement the vernacular folk architecture of the disparate parts of this country to create contemporary houses that will never seem dated.

The term Post-Modernism caught on as the name for all developments since the general exhaustion of modernism itself. . . . It told you what you were leaving without committing you to any particular destination.

—Tom Wolfe, *From Bauhaus to Our House,* 1981

11. NOVELTY AND DIVERGENCE 1960–1990s

A PERSONAL VIEW OF RECENT ARCHITECTURAL TRENDS

Since the early 1960s many architects have attempted with varying degrees of success to create a new "postmodern" architecture. C. Ray Smith's *Supermannerism—New Attitudes in Post-Modern Architecture* offers an articulate explanation of this phrase. Smith says that this new architecture of the sixties is characterized by "a systematic manipulation of established principles, its alteration of scale, its reordering of surface detail . . . expanded to include the vernacular, the anonymous, and such elements of our ordinary life or popular culture as comic books."*

It requires a considerable intellectual adjustment (at least for me) to leap from the underlying rationalism of modern architecture to such an arbitrary and capricious approach to design. The results are not just whimsical—that I could understand—they are simply perverse. Windows are often randomly placed with no consistency of pattern or even window type. They sometimes appear to have been bought at a jumble sale of odds and ends. (It is almost the same as hanging pictures in your house at odd locations and purposely off horizontal.) Details are apt to be self-consciously awkward as if put together by an inexperienced do-it-yourselfer rather than a master craftsman. Siding is often mismatched and combined in bizarre ways; shingles may be used on one wall and clapboard or occasionally cheap composition siding on another even when cost is not a primary factor. I have seen several instances where part of a house may actually be left unpainted as if the house was not yet finished. The studied awkwardness of this design philosophy is self-conscious and contrived.

Robert Venturi (b. 1925) was the standard-bearer for the legion of reformers who embraced this new fashion. It was an architecture that purported to be "inclusivistic," witty, and amusing and its proponents evocative, daring, and profound.

In lauding a Venturi house in Chestnut Hill, Pennsylvania, Smith wrote: "Inside, the most celebrated of his design jokes is a stair that leads to nowhere; it can be used as a large whatnot and as a ladder to

*Smith, C. Ray, *Supermannerism—New Attitudes in Post-Modern Architecture* (New York: Dutton, 1977).

aid in washing a window, but otherwise it has no function. It is, nevertheless, a gantry to the sky, an infinity stair that is a clear symbol of our age."

I believe I am as receptive as the next person to new ideas, but I have yet to be persuaded that I am missing something really important here. There is so much attention given to the novel, the quirky, and the slick that one has to remember that many dedicated, talented, and inventive architects simply do not subscribe to the gospel of Postmodernism or any other fad that happens to come along. There are counterparts today to the talented architects of the 1920s whom Mark Alan Hewitt described as working "quietly to create a large oeuvre almost unnoticed by anyone save their appreciative clients." In contrast to these professional men and women, there were others who "strutted society's stage like Tartuffes"—men who were the prototypes of "the avant-garde propagandist, the master of public relations, which the architect of today continues to emulate."*

Perhaps it is time to have some quietly competent, simple, livable houses again and give less adulation to buildings that strive desperately to be different in the mistaken belief that they are truly innovative. Originality comes from within a person, and a solution to an architectural problem is found in the nature of the problem itself. Too much recent architecture seems less concerned with complementing an existing community of buildings than standing apart with a patronizing air of condescension.

Even the words used to describe houses have changed. Houses are no longer charming, comfortable, livable, or homey; they are witty, amusing statements. But isn't wit inherently spontaneous? The quick retort, the sudden quip, and the zinger inevitably pale when given architectural permanence. It's like having to listen to the same wisecrack repeated ad infinitum.

Deconstructionism, the latest of the new fads, celebrates structures that are made to look like they are about to fall down. Perhaps it is the artist/architect commenting on the shortcomings of our society and a reflection of the hopeless prospects for the future. Should we as architects really reflect the problems in our social structure by designing chaotic-looking buildings? I think it is a lowering of standards at a time when positive leadership is needed.

*Hewitt, Mark Alan, *The Architect & the American Country House* (New Haven, CT: Yale University Press, 1990).

There is a chasm between self-styled avant-garde architects and the public. The essence of this gap was captured in a letter to the editor in the November 1992 issue of *The Atlantic* magazine, from a reader named Elizabeth Frazer: ". . . as I've come to expect from architects and their cohorts, function and utility lose out to form's designs, whims, and egos." She is not alone in her view.

It is an unfortunate impasse because this is a time when builders and architects should be working together more than they do. It is a time when factory-built housing is desperately needed and could benefit from creative contributions from competent architects who are concerned with creating simple, low-key designs that will blend together in cohesive communities and not always fight for attention to be the most distinctive and conspicuous of the lot. Is it really so gauche to find comfort in simple, unassertive surroundings that wear well in changing seasons and adapt to our moods throughout the course of our domestic lives? Mies's "Less is more" became "Less is a bore" in Postmodern parlance. An appropriate twist now might be "More is a bore."

There is a need today for responsible use of our remaining rural areas. Cluster or conservation zoning encourages the preservation of open space to the benefit of the developer and the community. One need only visit the hamlets in the English Cotswolds to see how effective clustering can be. It has worked for hundreds of years in Britain and still sets a worthy standard.

Unfortunately, most houses we live in today are badly planned, devoid of inherent character, and deficient in fundamental design. The 1980s saw a plethora of pretentious monstrosities that "upscale" developers think will attract buyers by a blatant "curb appeal." The new proliferation of witty statements by trendy architects can be just as offensive. In fact, I'm not sure which is the more grating of the two. But I have more faith in the American public and believe there is another way.

What is the answer? Let me use the analogy of language. There are several helpful books on how to write effectively: William Zinsser's *On Writing Well*, Clarkson Potter's *Writing for Publication*, and of course Strunk and White's *The Elements of Style*. They all give the same advice and admonishment: Writing is communication. We write effectively when we write concisely, clearly, and succinctly. We should avoid adverbs when a terse verb works, favor the active tense and not the passive, and avoid business jargon and trendy clichés. Writing style—that personal touch—evolves in good writers by their effective use of the English language. If you have something to say, say it crisply and simply so the meaning will be clear and the text fun to read.

The analogy should be evident. There is a language of architecture, and structures should say what they mean. The Gothic cathedral, for example, is simple in that there is almost nothing superfluous or extraneous in its design. All elements are defined and emphasized by the articulation of the structure. When the more floral embellishments of the tracery disguise the structural system, the style overwhelms the substance and the building loses clarity and definition. It loses that power and strength which derives from the celebration of its essence. Words like "honest," "cohesive," "unity," and "straightforward" should still have a place when discussing architecture, and a deference to natural surroundings and community is still appropriate.

In the 1980s our colloquial expressions lost vigor and snap. "Like" and "ya know" are endemic in our vernacular and the near future doesn't look promising. People with little or nothing to say try to disguise that fact by the use of excessive verbiage. Ask any teacher who corrects written examinations!

Much of the architecture of the eighties was a visual equivalent of verbosity. "Ya know, like, let's use a column. It doesn't have to do anything, but let's just use it." "Better yet, lest anyone think we wanted to use a column of a recognizable order, let's distort its proportions and shape it so grotesquely—maybe even just make a silhouette out of plywood and now we can really show our disdain for the public, sneer at the past, and be comforted that we have made a statement worthy of our era."

It is my hope that the houses built in the coming years will be simpler and less pretentious than we saw in the eighties. Houses should have more substance than style; plans should be more thoroughly developed than the ones in most plan books or than most developers offer to the public. The character of houses should be less self-conscious and less intrusive than most architects produce today.

Throughout our history, our best houses have derived elegance from simplicity, dignity from restraint, and richness from subtle diversity. There should always be a place in our communities for comfortable, livable houses that express the character of the region, the site, and the people who live in them. A good house has integrity of design rather than a jumbled collection of glitzy gimmicks. Let's not worry so much about what particular style our houses are; let's trust that they will simply have style—an inherent, intrinsic style that derives from the nature of the materials used and an expression of the spaces defined. Above all, let's build houses that live comfortably with their surroundings, are courteous to their neighbors, and are deferential to the environment. I believe our American houses can continue to provide the comfort and sense of well-being that they have in the past. The need to show off will be less important to a society that is increasingly comfortable with itself, one that is enriched by a knowledge of our history and a greater appreciation of our architectural heritage.

Katonah, New York

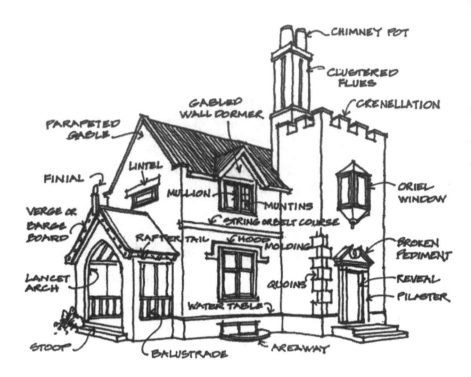

Some architectural terms found in the glossary

GLOSSARY

adobe: an Arabic word for the sun-dried clay bricks used by the Spanish in the Southwest. The Indian structures were sun-dried clay as well but were usually not in the form of bricks.

arcade: a series of arches supported by columns or piers.

architrave: 1) the lowest of the three parts of a classical entablature. 2) the exterior casing or molding around a window or door.

art nouveau: a style of decoration and architectural detail popular in the 1890s featuring sinuous, floral motifs.

ashlar: a kind of smooth-faced stone masonry with even horizontal and vertical joints.

astylar: a building without columns or pilasters.

balloon frame: a structural system or framework evolved about 1830 using standardized lightweight lumber where 2-by-4 studs extended from foundation to roof. Supposedly invented in Chicago by George Washington Snow, it replaced cumbersome heavy timber and braced framing and was made possible by the availability of inexpensive nails. After the Second World War it was generally replaced by the western or platform frame which was constructed one story at a time.

baluster: a post or spindle supporting a handrail on a stairs or balcony railing.

balustrade: a section of low "fencing" consisting of intermittent supporting posts and horizontal rails with balusters or crossbars in between.

barge-board: a board, often elaborately carved, attached to the projecting edge of a gable roof. Also called a verge-board. Common to the Gothic Revival, Elizabethan, and Tudor styles.

Baroque: the late phase of Renaissance architecture which originated in Italy in the early 1600s and spread throughout Europe. It is characterized by its energetic, curvalinear, and grandiose design.

batter: the slight inward slope sometimes given to a wall, tower, or pier.

bay: a projected portion of a building, as in a bay window. Also the distance or span between two principal column lines or framing members.

bay window: a window or band of windows that projects from the face of a building within a structural bay.

STRUCTURAL TERMS

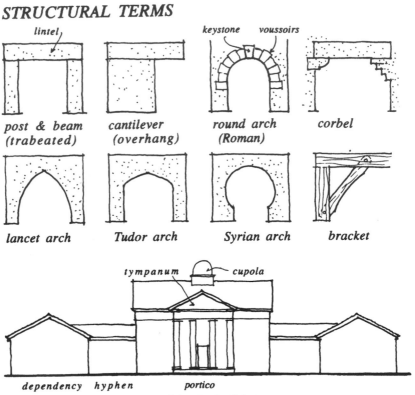

lintel

keystone   voussoirs

post & beam
(trabeated)

cantilever
(overhang)

round arch
(Roman)

corbel

lancet arch

Tudor arch

Syrian arch

bracket

tympanum   cupola

dependency   hyphen   portico

FIVE PART PALLADIAN COMPOSITION

BRICK BOND

common

English

Flemish

STONE

dressed

ashlar

cobble

SIDING

clapboard

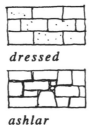

board & batten

quoins

pilasters

belt-course: a horizontal band on the facade of a building, usually indicating the floor level behind it. Also called a string course, it is sometimes placed just below the windows.

belvedere: a pavilion or building constructed as a place to enjoy an engaging view. It can be anything from a gazebo in a small garden to Palladio's Villa Capra (page 38).

berm: an earth embankment placed against a masonry foundation wall, or simply an elongated mound of earth.

beveled siding: horizontal overlapping boards that are thinner at the top than they are at the bottom. (See clapboard.)

blind arch: a shallow, windowless niche or recess in a wall that is defined by an arch.

braced frame: a system of timber framing incorporating the major components of heavy timber framing at corners as well as the tops and bottoms of walls but depending on long diagonal braces at the outside corners for lateral stability. Knee braces are eliminated and lighter weight studs are used approximately two feet on center as intermediary structural supports.

bracket: any strut or angled support of a shelf, beam, overhang, or projecting roof.

bracket capital: a heavy, squared timber making a tee on top of a timber post extending a foot or so under the girder which it supports. Found in the Spanish Southwest where they were often embellished with decorative curves.

broken pediment: a classical pediment which does not close at the top. It was a feature of Baroque architecture and was incorporated into some late Stuart and Georgian work.

bungalow: a one-story house with large overhangs and a dominating roof. Generally in the Craftsman style, it originated in California in the 1890s. The prototype was a house used by British Army officers in India in the nineteenth century. From the Hindi word *bangala* meaning "of Bengal."

buttress: a masonry projection from a wall to add strength and to resist the outward thrust of a roof or vault above.

campanile: a bell tower usually attached to or near a church.

canales: (Spanish) projecting gutters or spouts built to carry rainwater away from the face of a building. Prominent in Pueblo style houses.

cantilever: a projecting or overhanging beam, slab, or portion of a building with no visible means of support.

ARCHITECTURAL TERMS

ROOF TYPES

gable

gambrel

hip(ped)

mansard

*parapeted
gable*

*Flemish or
Dutch gable*

*cross
gable*

shed

WINDOWS

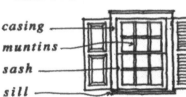

head

casing
muntins
sash
sill

double-hung

transom light

transom

mullion

stile

rail

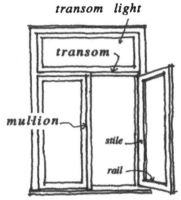

casements with transom

awning

hopper

*Palladian or
Venetian window*

oriel

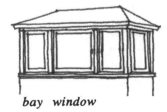

bay window

capital: the top part of a classical column. (*See* entablature.)

cartouche: a fancy oval or oblong decorative device usually embellished with swags or garlands.

casement window: an operating window hinged on one side which swings either in or out (usually out).

cement: a powder of calcined (burned) rock or stone used to make concrete. Portland cement was first made in Portland, England.

clapboard: (pronounced "kla-bord") overlapping horizontal boards used as siding on wood-framed houses. It is often wedge shaped with the narrower edge along the top and is called beveled siding. In England it is called weatherboarding.

classical: referring to the formal architectural style of ancient Greece or Rome or to the styles which derived from these prototypes.

clerestory: (pronounced "clear-story") a series of windows placed high in a wall. Evolved from the Gothic churches where the clerestory appeared above the aisle roofs.

cobble: (cobblestone) a naturally rounded, uncut stone usually eight to twelve inches in diameter.

column: a supporting post, generally round. In classical orders the column consists of base, shaft, and capital (page 42).

common bond: brickwork where a row of headers is placed between five or six courses of stretchers. (*See* Flemish bond.)

concrete: a mixture of cement, water, sand, and stones (called aggregate) which hardens to a stonelike consistency.

console: a small bracketlike member placed at the soffit of a cornice or roof overhang. Implies a double or shallow S curve in profile.

Contemporary: any modern house that derives its character from the nature of its own materials and structure rather than from traditional or derivative stylistic expressions.

corbel: a projecting stone or a succession of stone or brick projecting from a masonry wall which supports a beam, shelf, or balcony.

Corinthian order: the most elaborate of the classical orders (page 41).

cornice: the upper portion of a classical entablature. Also the projecting decorative molding placed at the top of a wall or pillar or at the eave line of a roof. (*See* entablature.)

corona: the horizontal member just below the crown molding in a classical entablature. (*See* entablature.)

cottage orné: a rustic, romantic Victorian house using tree trunks and branches as columns and brackets.

course: the continuous level range of brick or masonry throughout the face or faces of a building.

crenellation: the notched parapet or battlements at the top of a castle wall.

cross-gabled: front- and rear-facing gables at right angles to the main axis of an end-gabled building.

crown molding: the cymarecta cap molding at the top of a classical cornice (page 39).

cupola: a small turretlike structure projecting above a building's roof. Usually glazed but can be louvered. (*See* lantern.)

cymarecta: the double-curved crown molding that often caps a classical cornice. (*See* entablature.)

cymatium: the crown molding that caps a classical cornice (often a cymarecta).

dentils: small rectangular blocks placed in a row, like teeth, as part of a classical cornice. (*See* entablature.)

dependency: an outbuilding or wing of a house usually connected to the main house by a hyphen that forms part of a five-part composition promoted by Palladio.

Doric order: the earliest and simplest of the classical orders (page 40).

dormer: a glazed structure with its own roof that projects from the main roof of a building or is a continuation of the upper part of a wall so that the eave line is interrupted by the dormer.

double-hung window: a pair of superimposed wooden sashes that are offset so as to slide up and down within the same frame. Called a sash window in Britian.

Dutch gable: a masonry gable that extends above the roof as a parapet and is either stepped or given a fanciful curved profile. Also called a Flemish gable.

eave: the lower edge of a roof which projects beyond the face of the wall.

egg and dart molding: a decorative molding in classical cornices that resembles alternating egg-shaped ovals with downward-pointing darts.

English bond: brickwork where each course alternates between one row of headers and one row of stretchers. (*See* Flemish bond and common bond.)

entablature: the top portion on a classical order supported by columns which forms the base for the pediment. It consists of the architrave, the frieze, and the cornice (page 41).

CLASSICAL
ARCHITECTURAL
TERMS

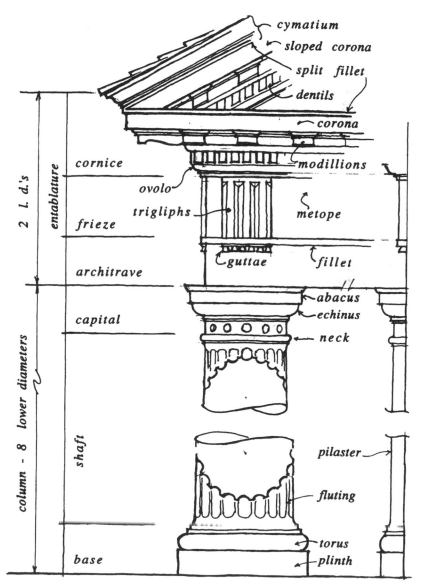

cymatium
sloped corona
split fillet
dentils
corona

cornice
modillions
ovolo
trigliphs
metope
frieze
architrave
guttae
fillet
abacus
echinus
capital
neck

entablature
2 l. d.'s

shaft
pilaster
fluting

column - 8 lower diameters

torus
plinth
base

entasis: the slight inward curve or taper given to the upper two-thirds of a classical column.

eyebrow dormer: an arched roof dormer with no side walls; the roof simply curves to follow the arch of the window.

facade: the front or principal elevation of a building. Sometimes other elevations are called facades, but the term usually refers to the front.

fanlight: a semicircular or elliptical transom window above a doorway. Introduced in the Federal period, it is an identifying feature of the Federal or Adamesque house.

fascia: the finish board which covers the ends of roof rafters.

fenestration: the window openings of a building. Often includes exterior door openings as well.

festoon: a carved loop or garland of leaves and flowers suspended between two points, used to embellish or decorate a building.

fillet: a small square molding directly above the corona and the crown molding on a classical cornice. When there is a pediment the fillet is "hinged" or "split"—one horizontal along the horizontal corona and one diagonal between the crown molding and the sloping corona of the cornice.

finial: a decorative ornament affixed to the top of any pointed roof or architectural feature.

Flemish bond: a distinctive pattern of brickwork where the headers (ends of the brick) alternate with the stretchers (sides of the brick) and where each course is staggered so that a header is always centered above and below a stretcher. Common in Georgian buildings both here and in England. (See English bond and common bond.)

Flemish gable: *see* Dutch gable.

fluting: the parallel, vertical, concave grooves incised along the length of a column. The Tuscan column was actually the only order to omit fluting.

foliated: floral decoration, specifically the use of leaves.

folly: a whimsical or romantic structure built with no utility other than to enhance a garden or view. Popular in the eighteenth and nineteenth centuries as gazebos, grottos, and even ruins. From the French *folie* meaning delight or favorite abode rather than the commom use of the word meaning foolish or stultified effort.

four-square: the name given to the simple, square-shaped house built in profusion as middle-class housing between 1900 and 1930.

frieze: the middle section of a classical entablature—between the architrave and the cornice (pages 40—41). It is also the name of any long, horizontal section at the top of a wall just below the ceiling, or the eave line if it is exterior.

gable: the triangular portion of a wall defined by the sloping edges of the roof and a horizontal line between the eave line. Can also be a gabled dormer.

gable roof: a pitched roof that ends in a gable.

gambrel roof: a ridged roof having two slopes on each side where the lower slope is steeper than the upper.

garrison colonial: a neo-colonial revival of the Early New England Colonial clapboard house featuring the jetted or overhanging second floor and usually diamond paned windows.

grade: the ground level around a building.

hacienda: (Spanish) an estate devoted to agriculture. A *rancho* would be comparable but devoted to stock raising.

half-timber: a timber-framed building where the infill of nogging or wattle and daub is left exposed to the weather as opposed to being covered by clapboards as was common in New England.

head: the top section of a window, door, or other opening.

hip: the sloping ridge formed by the intersection of two adjacent roof planes.

hipped roof: a roof comprised of four or more sloping planes that all start at the same level.

home: an occupied primary resident or dwelling place.

hood molding: a molding placed above a window or door that turns downward at the end and then turns horizontal again for a very short distance. Common to Gothic buildings or styles that evolved from the medieval era. Also called a drip molding.

hopper window: an inswinging window hinged at the bottom.

horseshoe arch: an arch shaped like a horseshoe—common in Syria and the Far East. Appears in Exotic Revival houses in the 1850s—1880s. Also called a Syrian arch.

house: a building constructed as a residence or dwelling.

hyphen: the portion of a five-part Palladian composition that connects the main central block to the two flanking dependencies.

Ionic order: the second of the classical orders (page 41).

jamb: the sides of a door, arch, or window opening.

jetty: the overhanging cantilever or projection of an upper story in front of the facade of the story below it.

knee or knee brace: a short diagonal framing member in timber-frame construction connecting a vertical post with a horizontal beam and by triangulation makes the connection laterally stable.

lally column: a concrete-filled pipe column.

lancet arch: a pointed arch, characteristic of Gothic architecture.

lantern: another term for a cupola.

leaded glass: a window comprised of small panes of glass held together by lead strips called cames.

lean-to: a shedlike structure with a single sloping roof built against a house or barn.

light: a pane of glass, as in a window light, or the whole sash, as in a skylight.

lintel: a load-bearing beam which spans a door or window opening.

loggia: a pillared gallery or porch open on at least one side. Usually an integral part of the building's mass rather than an appended porch.

mansard roof: a roof having two slopes on all four sides. The lower slope can be curved but is always close to vertical and the upper slope is always close to horizontal. Named for the French architect François Mansart (1598–1666) but popular in the Second Empire style of the 1850s. (The English consider a mansard roof synonymous with a gambrel roof which has a double-sloped roof on two sides rather than on all four.)

masonry: stone, brick, or concrete block construction.

medallion: a round or oval-shaped decorative device used in plastered ceilings but also used as an embellishment on the exterior of elaborate Baroque buildings.

modern: a house built with twentieth-century skills and materials. Usually means contemporary but could be a modern reproduction.

modernistic: a derogatory term for a copy or imitation contemporary. Particularly pertinent to Moderne buildings of the 1920s and 1930s.

modillion: a small ornamental bracket used in series in the cornice of the Corinthian and Composite orders.

mortise and tenon: a joint or connection in wood construction consisting of a squared-off cavity (mortise) made to receive a projection on the end of a piece of wood (tenon).

mullion: a vertical post, frame, or double jamb dividing two window sashes or large panes of fixed glass. Not to be confused with muntin.

muntins: the cross pieces dividing the panes of glass within a window sash. Often incorrectly called mullions.

nave: the large central volume of a church or cathedral flanked by side aisles. From the Latin *navis* for ship or naval.

nogging: the brick infilling between the timbers of a timber-framed building.

octagon: an eight-sided building usually with a hipped roof popularized by Orson Squire Fowler in the 1850s. (See page 78.)

order: any of several specific styles of classical architecture.

oriel window: a bay window on an upper floor usually associated with late medieval buildings.

orné: see cottage orné.

Palladian: the architectural interpretation of classical architecture by Italian Renaissance architect Andrea Palladio (1508–1580), or any classical style based on his work. Lord Burlington and Colen Campbell established Palladianism as the principal English style in the first half of the eighteenth century. It had an important influence on the course of American colonial architecture in the second half of the eighteenth century.

parapet: the extension of a masonry wall above the roof line.

parti: (pronounced "par-tee") the architect's resolution of a design concept—a basic layout. All the designs in this guide have the same parti.

patio: (Spanish) an open courtyard. The word has come to mean almost any ground-level area used for outdoor living.

pediment: the triangular gable defined by the crown molding at the edge of a gabled roof and the horizontal line between the eaves.

pent: a small shed roof attached to the wall of a house without brackets. Common in Pennsylvania.

pergola: an arbor or open structure constructed of wood and serving as a framework upon which vines grow.

piazza: an obsolete term for a broad verandah.

Picturesque: the romantic styles of architecture usually associated with most of the Victorian era based on the seventeenth-century paintings that idealized man's relationship to nature.

pilaster: a flat rectangular column attached to the face of a building— usually at the corners—or as a frame at the sides of a doorway.

pitch: the slope of a roof, usually given in degrees or as a ratio of height to a base of twelve—as in a 4 to 12 or a 6 in 12 pitch or 4:12 or 6:12.

plate: the horizontal framing member at the top of a wall.

plinth: the projecting base or block of a wall or column.

podium: a low wall or base serving as a platform for a building.

porch: a covered platform, usually with its own roof, attached to a building serving as a covered entryway or as a covered living area. (See verandah.)

portal: a doorway or entrance gateway.

porte cochere: a covered entrance porch for carriages, called a carport since the introduction of the automobile.

portico: a roofed entrance usually with columns.

pueblo: a communal building made of adobe by the Indians in the Southwest.

quoin: the dressed or finished stones at the corners of a masonry building. Sometimes faked in wooden or stucco buildings.

rafter: a sloping roof beam.

rail: a horizontal frame of a door, window sash, or panel. (A vertical frame is called a stile.)

rake: the slope or pitch of the gable end of a roof or rafter.

Renaissance architecture: the styles of architecture based on classical prototypes which evolved in Italy in the fifteenth century and spread throughout Europe in the following three hundred years. It culminated in the late eighteenth century with the Georgian architecture of the British colonies in North America.

reveal: the side wall next to a recessed door or window.

ridge: the horizontal line formed by the juncture of two sloping roof planes.

riser: the vertical surface of a stair. (The horizontal surface is called a tread.)

rococo: the fanciful style of decorative interior architecture which evolved in France around 1720 during the reign of Louis XV.

rusticated: masonry cut in large rectangular blocks and set in deep joints, giving a bold and assertive accent.

saltbox: a house squarish in plan with two stories at the front and one story at the rear, having a short sloping roof on the front and a long sloping one on the back.

Syrian arch: see horseshoe arch.

tenon: see mortise and tenon.

terra cotta: a baked clay material similar to brick but usually shaped in the form of tiles, decorative panels, or sculpted nonstructural features.

timber frame: a structural framing system incorporating large wooden members cut from tree trunks and shaped into square or rectangular sections with mortise and tenon joints held together with wooden pegs called trenals (from "tree-nail"). The frame is laterally braced with strategically placed knee braces.

trabeated: a structure based on post and beam construction as opposed to arched or vaulted construction.

tracery: the decorative pattern of supporting mullions in a Gothic window.

transom: the horizontal divider separating a large lower window from a smaller window above it.

transom window: a window or light above a door or window.

tread: the horizontal surface of a stair. (The vertical surface is a riser.)

Tudor: the English architectural style of the sixteenth century.

turret: a circular or polygonal projecting bay or structure usually with a steep pointed roof.

Tuscan order: the simplest of the five Roman classical orders and the only one that has smooth columns rather than ones with fluting (page 40).

tympanum: the triangular area within the moldings of a pediment.

Usonia: Frank Lloyd Wright considered this a better name for the United States. It suggested United States of North America and obviated confusion with any country in South America or the Union of South Africa. He attributed the term to Samuel Butler though the word does not appear in any of his novels. Wright referred to his modest, flat-roofed houses of the late 1930s as his Usonian houses.

vault: an arched or domed structure.

verandah: a covered porch used for sitting and entertaining.

vernacular: regional architecture with no stylistic pretensions. Non-architected rural buildings.

viga: (Spanish) the projecting beam ends or roof rafters of a Spanish or Indian pueblo.

volute: the spiral scroll-shaped capitals of the Ionic order. Also the spiral curved terminus of a handrail.

voussoir: the wedge shaped stone or brick used to form an arch or vault.

wattle and daub: a mixture of sticks and clay used to fill the space between the structural members of a timber-framed structure.

weatherboard: an English term for clapboard or beveled siding.

SUGGESTIONS FOR FURTHER READING

1. GENERAL COMPREHENSIVE SURVEYS

Aslet, Clive. *The American Country House.* New Haven and London: Yale University Press, 1990.

Aslet, Clive, and Powers, Alan. *The National Trust Book of the English House.* New York: Viking, 1985.

Burchard, John Ely, and Bush-Brown, Albert. *The Architecture of America; A Social and Cultural History.* Boston: Little, Brown, 1961.

Cook, Olive. *The English Country House: An Art and a Way of Life.* London: Thames and Hudson, 1974.

Davidson, Marshall B. *Notable American Houses.* New York: American Heritage Publishing, 1971.

Downing, Antoinette F., and Scully, Vincent J., Jr. *The Architectural Heritage of Newport, Rhode Island, 1640–1915.* 2nd ed. New York: Clarkson N. Potter, 1967.

Foley, Mary Mix. *The American House.* New York: Harper & Row, 1980.

Girouard, Mark. *The Victorian Country House.* London: Oxford University Press, 1971.

Handlin, David P. *American Architecture.* New York: Thames and Hudson, 1985.

Historic American Buildings Survey, National Park Service, U.S. Department of the Interior. *What Style Is It? A Guide to American Architecture.* Washington, D.C.: The Preservation Press, 1983.

Jordan, R. Furneaux. *A Concise History of Western Architecture.* New York: Harcourt, Brace Jovanovich, 1984.

McAlester, Virginia, and McAlester, Lee. *A Field Guide to American Houses.* New York: Alfred A. Knopf, 1989.

Morrison, Hugh. *Early American Architecture.* New York: Oxford University Press, 1952; Dover Publications, 1987.

Moss, Roger W. *The American Country House.* New York: Henry Holt & Company, 1990.

Muthesius, Hermann. *The English House.* New York: Rizzoli, 1979. (Originally *Das englische Haus.* Berlin: 1904/5.)

Nicholson, Nigel. *The National Trust Book of Great Houses of Britain.* London: Granada Publishing, 1983.

Reid, Richard. *The Georgian House.* London: Bishopgate Press, 1989.

Rifkind, Carole. *A Field Guide to American Architecture.* New York: New American Library, 1980.

Risebero, Bill. *The Story of Western Architecture.* Cambridge, MA: MIT Press, 1979/85.

Roth, Leland M. *A Concise History of American Architecture.* New York: Harper & Row, 1979.

Stamp, Gavin, and Goulancourt, Andre. *The English House 1860–1914.* U.K.: Faber & Faber, 1986.

Sturgis, Frank E. *American Architecture: Westchester County, New York.* Croton-on-Hudson, NY: North River Press, 1977.

Whiffen, Marcus. *American Architecture Since 1781.* Cambridge, MA: MIT Press, 1969/92.

Walker, Lester. *American Shelter, an Illustrated Encyclopedia of the American House.* Woodstock, NY: Overlook Press, 1981.

2. EARLY COLONIAL

Cummings, Abbott Lowell. *The Framed House of Massachusetts Bay, 1625–1725.* Cambridge, MA, and London: Belknap Press of Harvard University Press, 1979.

Forman, H. Chandlee. *Early Manor Houses and Plantation Houses of Maryland.* 2nd ed. Baltimore: Bodine and Associates, 1982.

Forman, H. Chandlee. *Maryland Architecture: A Short History from 1634 Through the Civil War.* Cambridge, MD: Tidewater Publishers, 1968.

Isham, Norman M., and Brown, Albert F. *Early Connecticut Houses.* New York: Dover Publications, 1965.

Kelly, J. Frederick. *The Early Domestic Architecture of Connecticut.* New York: Dover Publications, 1924/63.

Schuler, Stanley. *Old New England Homes.* Exton, PA: Schiffer Publishing, 1984.

3. COLONIAL AND GEORGIAN

Ackerman, James S. *Palladio.* U.K.: Penguin Books, 1966.

Architects' Emergency Committee. *Great Georgian Houses of America.* 2 vols. New York: Dover Publications, 1933; 1937/70.

Howells, John Mead. *The Architectural Heritage of the Piscataqua.* (1937) New York: Architectural Book Publishing, 1965.

Mullins, Lisa C., ed. *Architectural Treasures of Early America.* 10 vols. Harrisburg, PA: National Historical Society, 1987.

Palladio, Andrea. *The Four Books of Architecture.* (1738) New York: Dover Publications.

Stoney, Samuel. *Plantations of the Carolina Lowlands.* New York: Dover Publications.

Whiffen, Marcus. *The Eighteenth-Century Houses of Williamsburg.* Charlottesville, VA: University of Virginia Press, 1984.

4. FEDERAL, NEOCLASSICAL, AND GREEK REVIVAL

Benjamin, Asher. *The American Builder's Companion* (1837). New York: Dover Publications.

Hamlin, Talbot. *Greek Revival in America.* New York: Dover Publications, 1944/64.

Kennedy, Roger G. *Architecture, Men, Women, and Money.* Cambridge, MA: MIT Press, 1989.

Kennedy, Roger G. *Greek Revival America.* New York: Stewart, Tabori & Chang, 1989.

5. PICTURESQUE AND NINETEENTH CENTURY

Davis, Alexander Jackson. *Rural Residences.* New York: New York University, 1837; DaCapo Press, 1980.

Downing, Andrew Jackson. *Architecture of Country Houses.* (1850) New York: Dover Publications, 1969.

Downing, Andrew Jackson. *Victorian Cottage Residences.* (1842) New York: Dover Publications, 1981.

Fowler, Orson Squire. *The Octagon House: A Home for All.* (185) New York: Dover Publications, 1953/73.

Girouard, Mark. *Sweetness and Light: The Queen Anne Movement, 1860–1900.* New Haven and London: Yale University Press, 1977.

Holmes, Kriston, and Watersun, David. *The Victorian Express.* Wilsonville, OR: Beautiful America Publishing, 1991.

Vaux, Calvert. *Villas & Cottages.* (1864) New York: Dover Publications, 1970.
Zukowsky, John, and Stimson, Robbe Pierce. *Hudson River Villas.* New York: Rizzoli, 1985.

6. INDIGENOUS STYLES

Brooks, H. Allen. *The Prairie School: Frank Lloyd Wright and His Midwest Contemporaries.* New York: W. W. Norton, 1972.
Lancaster, Clay. *The American Bungalow, 1880s–1920s.* New York: Abbeville Press, 1983.
Scully, Vincent J., Jr. *The Shingle Style.* New Haven: Yale University Press, 1955.
Stickley, Gustav. *Craftsman Homes.* (Also *More Craftsman Homes.*) New York: Dover Publications, 1979.
von Holst, H. V. *Country and Suburban Homes of the Prairie School Period.* New York: Dover Publications, 1913/82.

7. PALATIAL PALACES

Folsom, Merrill. *Great American Mansions and Their Stories.* New York: Hastings House, 1963.
Hunter, Julius K. *Westmoreland and Portland Places: The History and Architecture of America's Premier Streets, 1888–1988.* Columbia: University of Missouri Press, 1988.
Junior League of Greenwich. *The Great Estates, Greenwich, Connecticut, 1880–1930.* Canaan, NH: Phoenix Publishing, 1986.
Lewis, Arnold. *American Country Houses of the Gilded Age.* New York: Dover Publications, 1886–87/82.
Randall, Monica. *The Mansions of Long Island's Gold Coast.* New York: Hastings House, 1979.

8. REMINISCENT STYLES

Cortissoz, Royal. Introduction to *Domestic Architecture (A monograph of the work of Harrie T. Lindeberg).* New York: William Helburn, 1940.
Embury, Aymar II. *The Dutch Colonial House.* New York: McBride, Nast & Company, 1913.

Gowans, Alan. *The Comfortable House*. Cambridge, MA, and London: MIT Press, 1986.

Hewitt, Mark Alan. *The Architect & the American Country House 1890–1940*. New Haven and London: Yale University Press, 1990.

Hoffstot, Barbara. *Landmark Architecture of Palm Beach*. rev ed. Pittsburgh: Ober Park Associates, 1980.

Mellor Meigs & Howe. *Mellor Meigs & Howe: A Monograph*. New York: Architectural Book Publishing, 1923/92.

Morgan, Keith N. *Charles A. Platt: The Artist as Architect*. Cambridge, MA: MIT Press, 1985.

Parrish Art Museum. *The Long Island Country House 1870–1930*. Southampton, NY: The Parrish Art Museum, 1988.

Sclare, Liisa and Donald. *Beaux-Arts Estates—A Guide to the Architecture of Long Island*. New York: Viking Press, 1975/79.

9. MODERN ARCHITECTURE

Ford, James, and Morrow, Katherine. *The Modern House in America*. New York: Architectural Book Publishing, 1940.

Hitchcock, Henry-Russell, and Johnson, Philip. *The International Style*. New York: W. W. Norton, 1932/66.

Hitchcock, Henry-Russell, and Drexler, Arthur. *Built in USA: Post-War Architecture*. New York: Museum of Modern Art, 1952.

Joedicke, Jurgen. *The History of Modern Architecture*. New York: Frederick Praeger, 1959.

Kaufman, Edgar. *Fallingwater, A Frank Lloyd Wright Country House*. New York: Abbeville Press, 1986.

Mock, Elizabeth B. *If You Want to Build a House*. New York: Museum of Modern Art, 1946.

Pevsner, Nikolaus. *Pioneers of Modern Design*. New York: Museum of Modern Art, 1949.

Sergeant, John. *Frank Lloyd Wright's Usonian Houses: The Case for Organic Architecture*. New York: Whitney Library of Design—an imprint of Watson-Guptill Publications, 1976.

Wolfe, Tom. *From Bauhaus to Our House*. New York: Farrar, Straus & Giroux, 1981.

Wright, Frank Lloyd. *The Natural House*. New York: Horizon Press, 1954.

10. POSTMODERNISM

Jencks, Charles. *The Language of Post-Modern Architecture*. New York: Rizzoli International Publications, 1977/84.

Moore, Charles, Allen, Gerald, and Lyndon, Donlyn. *The Place of Houses*. New York: Holt, Rinehart & Winston, 1974.

Scully, Vincent, Jr. *The Shingle Style Today or The Historian's Revenge*. New York: George Braziller, 1974.

Smith, C. Ray. *Supermannerism: New Attitudes in Post-Modern Architecture*. New York: E. P. Dutton, 1977.

Venturi, Robert. *Complexity and Contradiction in Architecture*. (1966) New York: Museum of Modern Art, 1977.

11. SPECIAL

Baker, John Milnes, AIA. *How to Build a House with an Architect*. New York: Harper & Row, 1977/88.

Dunn, Alan. *Architecture Observed*. (laugh lines by America's foremost cartoon critic) New York: Architectural Record Books, 1971.

Lynes, Russell. *The Tastemakers*. New York: Dover Publishing, 1980.

National Trust for Historic Preservation. *Masterbuilders: A Guide to Famous American Architects*. Washington, DC: Preservation Press, 1985.

Raskin, Eugene. *Architecturally Speaking*. New York: Bloch Publishing, 1954/66.

Raskin, Eugene. *Architecture and People*. Englewood Cliffs, NJ: Prentice Hall, 1974.

Rybczynski, Witold. *Home: A Short History of an Idea*. New York: Viking Penguin, 1986.

Smith, A. G. *The American House Styles Coloring Book*. New York: Dover Publications, 1983.

INDEX